P9-CRW-623

CITY SECRETS

LONDON

ROBERT KAHN

SERIES EDITOR

TIM ADAMS

EDITOR

THE LITTLE BOOKROOM

NEW YORK

11
7
5
6
4
1
10
2
3

LONDON

1 Trafalgar Square, Soho & Covent Garden
2 St. James's, Westminster & Embankment
3 Hyde Park & Chelsea
4 Oxford Street & Mayfair
5 Regent's Park & Camden Town
6 Bloomsbury & King's Cross
7 Islington & Clerkenwell
8 The City
9 The South Bank
10 Notting Hill & The West
11 Hampstead & The North
12 The East End & Beyond
13 South of the River

Series Editor: Robert Kahn
Editor: Tim Adams
Assistant Editor: Lexy Bloom
Book Design: Katy Homans with Christine M. Moog, Homans Design
Original series and imprint design by Red Canoe, Deer Lodge, TN,
Caroline Kavanagh and Deb Koch
Maps: Jenny King
Key: Based on a design courtesy of E. R. Butler & Co., New York
Chapter divider pages: *Up and Down the London Streets*, by Mark Lemon.
London: Chapman and Hall, 1867. Courtesy Ursus Books Ltd., New York,
New York
Cover: Thomas Bowles (c.1712–c.1760) South West Prospect of London.
Engraving. Victoria & Albert Museum, London/Art Resource, New York

First Printing: October 2001
Printed in Hong Kong by South China Printing Company (1988) Ltd.

Library of Congress Cataloging-in-Publication Data
London / Robert Kahn, series editor.
p. cm. – (City secrets ; 3)
Includes bibliographical references and indexes.
ISBN 1-892145-07-3
1. Art, English–England–London–Guidebooks. 2. London (England)-
Guidebooks. 3. Celebrities–Homes and haunts–England–London–Guidebooks.
I. Kahn, Robert, 1950–
II. Series.

N6770 .L649 2001
914.2104'86–dc21

2001029675

Published by The Little Bookroom
5 St. Luke's Place
New York NY 10014
(212) 691-3321
(212) 691-2011 fax
book-room@rcn.com
editoral@citysecrets.com
www.citysecrets.com
Distributed by Publishers Group West; in the UK by Macmillan Distribution Ltd.

HOW TO USE THIS BOOK

This is a highly subjective guidebook which reflects the personal tastes and insights of its contributors. Our editors asked architects, painters, writers, and other cultural figures—many of them associated with the Sir John Soane's Museum, the Whitechapel Gallery or the Museum of London—to recommend an overlooked or underappreciated site or artwork, or, alternatively, one that is well-known but about which they could offer fresh insights, personal observations, or specialized information. Respondents were also invited to describe strolls, neighborhoods, events, shops, and all manner of idiosyncratic and traditional ways of spending time in London. These recommendations have been organized into 13 areas of London. Each area has an accompanying map, keyed to the text by numbers. The numbers appear in lozenges **3.9** and include an item number and a map number (which is also the chapter number). For example, a lozenge with the number 3.9 denotes item number 9 from Chapter 3, which appears on Map 3.

In addition, three icons appear throughout the book to reference restaurants 🍴, shops 🎁 and underground stations ⊖.

The editors are delighted with the high number of unusual and delightful "secrets" included here. At the same time, we acknowledge that London provides endlessly rich experiences, and that this book, though full, is not exhaustive. It is our hope that you will be inspired by the enthusiasm of our contributors to explore even further and discover secrets of your own, and when you do, let us know. We would love to hear about your city secrets—in any city, anywhere.

Finally, every care has been taken to ensure the accuracy of the information in this book. However, the publisher and the series editor are not able to accept responsibility for any consequences arising from use of the guide or the information it contains.

TABLE OF CONTENTS

PREFACE

When I was working on this book, I occasionally had in mind a particular short story by Robert Louis Stevenson. The story tells of a young man who, visiting a large city (not unlike London) for the first time, stumbles through a door in an unpromising side street and finds himself in a secret walled garden. The garden is full of the most extraordinary plants and flowers and there is a party going on to which the young man is welcomed. He is offered wonderful food and wine, makes new friends, falls in love. The next day he plans to visit the walled garden again, but, try as he might—it is a sad story—he can never find the door in the side street, and the city becomes foreign to him once more. The story seemed a little parable of what we all hope when we visit new cities: we hope to become insiders, to have access to a version of what London cab-drivers call "the knowledge:" an intimate geography of the kinds of places that make the city come fully alive. In a city as vast and accidental as London, this kind of knowledge is only ever partial and often eccentric. The idea of this book was a simple one, then: to gather together a selection of such highly personal impressions from a number of people who know the city best and love it most—notably its writers and its artists, its architects and its historians—and to build an anecdotal guide to London's best-kept secrets. The response was, in many ways, exhilarating. Everyone we invited to contribute, it seemed, had a favourite corner table—or a street or building or park or shop, which held for them special significance. Moreover—perhaps surprisingly—most were more than willing to share these haunts with discriminating strangers. The result, we hope, is an insight into the London that Londoners might carry in their heads. Though most familiar landmarks are represented, if somewhat obliquely, this book does not pretend to be comprehensive: rather it aims to open the door to a city no one has told you about before.

Tim Adams
London, April 2001

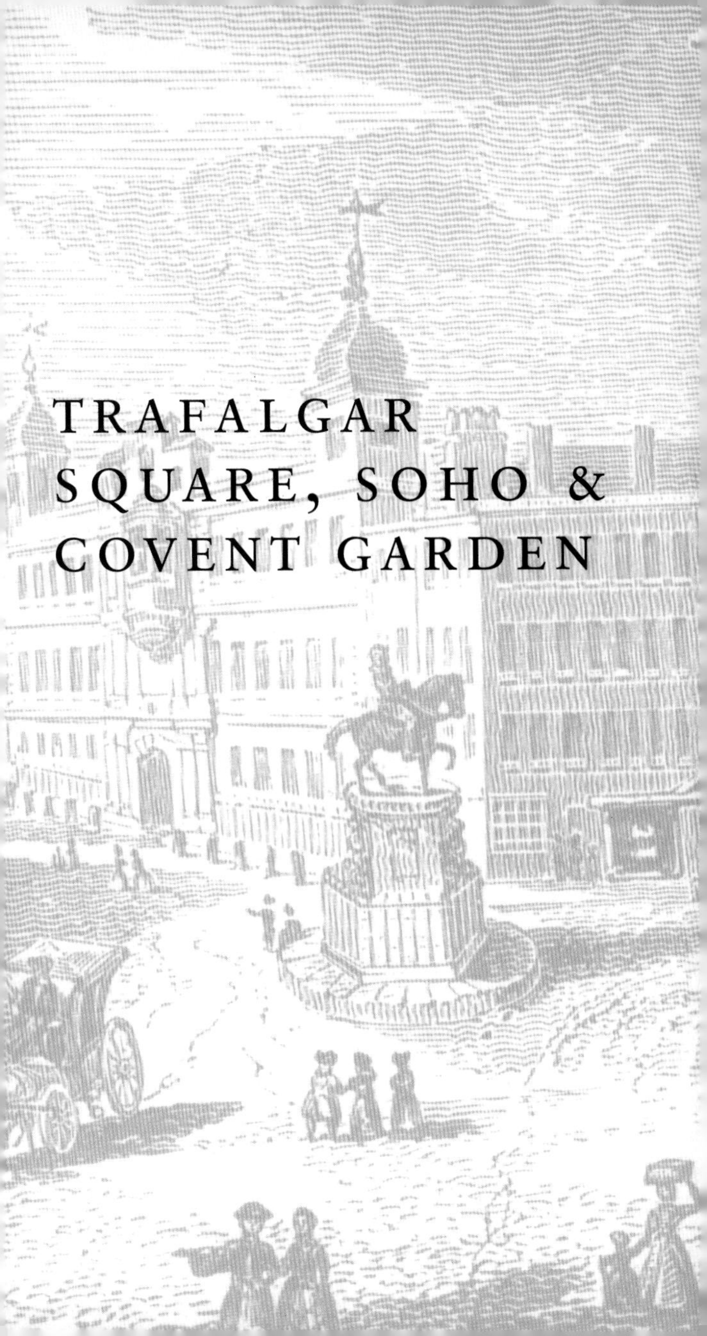

TRAFALGAR SQUARE, SOHO & COVENT GARDEN

TRAFALGAR SQUARE, SOHO & COVENT GARDEN

1. Statue of King Charles I
2. National Gallery
3. St. Martin-in-the-Fields Church
4. Post Office
5. National Portrait Gallery
6. Gordon's Wine Bar
7. The Adelphi
8. Somerset House
9. The Royal Opera House
10. Donmar Warehouse
11. Monmouth Coffee Company
12. Portwine's

13 Denmark Street
14 Hanway Street
15 French Protestant Church
16 House of St. Barnabas
17 Manette House
18 Kettners
19 Maison Bertaux
20 Notre Dame de France
21 Bar Italia
22 Andrew Edmunds
23 Air Street
24 Golden Nugget (see p. 75)
25 French House (see p. 186)

TRAFALGAR SQUARE, SOHO & COVENT GARDEN

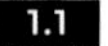

Statue of King Charles I

1633, Hubert Le Seuer
Trafalgar Square WC2
Charing Cross

The statue of Charles I is arguably the finest, most striking and most evocative of all London statues. However, very few of the thousands who pass it every day pause to admire it on its island site, let alone know of its long and colourful history. It is the work of Hubert Le Seuer and dates from 1633. It was not erected in its present location until about 1675, having been sold under Cromwell to a brazier who, with a shrewd eye to later financial advantage, buried it until the Restoration though he was ordered to destroy it. The statue predates Trafalgar Square itself by some 150 years and is one of the oldest remaining features of this part of London. It is prominent in one of the earliest known photographs of London, taken in 1838 when the statue was already two hundred years old. During the Second World War it was removed, and upon its return in 1947 it was given a new sword to replace the one which had disappeared in 1867. Each year on the 30th of January at 11am a wreath-laying takes place at the statue to commemorate the execution of the King on that day in 1649.

PETER HORROCKS
Barrister

1.2

National Gallery

Trafalgar Square WC2, 020 7747 2885
Charing Cross

Perhaps the most visited building in London, but not to be omitted for that reason. It is the world's most magisterial collection of European Painting. Less rubbish than in either

the Uffizi or the Louvre. The Sainsbury Wing (disliked by modernist architects but decorated in convincing reproduction of Florentine *pietra santa*) houses an unequalled collection of Italian art—from early Sienese to mannerism. Most user-friendly, visible gallery in Europe.
PETER PORTER
Poet

Supper at Emmaus

1600–1601, Caravaggio

No visit to London would be complete without a climb up the grand central staircase of the National Gallery, and a brief wander through stately rooms and glass doorways to the heart of the Baroque, and to Caravaggio.

To stand in front of this painting is to enter an ordinary home in Rome around the year 1600. The torn clothes, the simple food, table and chairs bring that very different world to immediate and vivid life. But this is no ordinary home. The drama as the apostles suddenly recognize the resurrected Jesus leaps out of the painting. One spreads his arms wide, almost reaching out of the canvas; the other grips the arms of his chair, about to rise in amazement. As you look, the textures and the colours that Caravaggio has created—the wood, the meat, the cloth, the muted green and brown—gradually bring the scene into recognizable reality. You leave, aware once again, of the possibility of the miraculous amidst everyday life.
THEODORE RABB
Historian

RECOMMENDED READING
Howard Hibbard, *Caravaggio*, Harper Collins, 1985.

The Arnolfini Wedding

1434, Jan van Eyck

A trip to London cannot be complete without a pilgrimage to Jan van Eyck's *The Arnolfini Wedding* in the galleries of Early Netherlandish Paintings at the National Gallery. I am always surprised by this jewel of a painting's small size and intense colours since long ago the image was imprinted in my brain by Howard McP. Davis at Columbia University through an in-depth elucidation of the painting before a projection of a large black-and-white glass slide.

Scholars dispute the function of the painting and the possible meanings of the shoes, the dog, the orange on the windowsill, and even the identity of the couple, but I would venture that few would argue about the chills that can be sent down your spine by the inscription *"Johannes ab eyck fuit hic"* ("Jan van Eyck was present") on the back wall and the tiny reflection of the artist himself at this event in the mirror.

NADINE ORENSTEIN
Curator

1.3 St. Martin-in-the-Fields Church

1682–1754

Trafalgar Square WC2, 020 7766 1100

Charing Cross

Cafe in the Crypt

020 7839 4342

Brass Rubbing Centre

020 7930 9306

St. Martin's is a beautiful church, but the basement is where we spent time every day we were in London. One can get sandwiches and soup (it was very cold when we were there). One can use the bathroom. And adjacent to these amenities is a workshop, open to the public, where one can buy paper and crayons and make rubbings of a wonderful collection of carvings and woodblocks.

LYNDA SCHOR
Author and teacher

Trafalgar Square Afternoon

⊖ Charing Cross

1.3 **St. Martin-in-the-Fields Church**
Trafalgar Square WC2, ☎ 020 7766 1100

1.4 **Post Office**
24–28 William IV Street WC2, ☎ 020 7484 9304

1.5 **National Portrait Gallery**
2 St. Martin's Place WC2, ☎ 020 7306 0055

Everyone has heard recordings of music performed by the Academy of St. Martin-in-the-Fields. In London, you have a chance to visit the actual church and hear a free performance. (Recitals are offered several afternoons a week and donations are at the visitor's discretion—check a daily paper for performers and times.) Afterwards, be certain to go downstairs to the crypt where you will walk over marked graves as you buy an inexpensive but tasty lunch in the cafeteria (see Cafe in the Crypt, at left). On some days, a small open-air market is held at the back of the church where jewelery, posters, and other quirky items are sold. Near the church (on the same street, leading into Charing Cross Road) is a post office where you can buy stamps—and not just for mailing cards home, either. British stamps honour authors and events, and are wonderfully handsome. A set can be framed. (I have the four stamps commemorating comic poet Edward Lear, each with a reproduction of one of his drawings and a line or two of his text, hanging over my writing desk.) And finally, cross the street and go into possibly the most interesting museum in all of London or England—the National Portrait Gallery. Here are portraits, some formal, some caricatures, some photographs and even sculptures of the most significant people in British history: royalty, rock stars, writers, actors, sports figures and prime ministers. This small area can keep you occupied, entertained and fed for at least half a day.

JOHANNA HURWITZ
Children's book writer

A Giant's Wedding

Half way through the writing of my novel about the Canadian giantess, Anna Swan, I found myself on the steps of St. Martin-in-the-Fields (see p. 14), imagining her June wedding in 1871 to her giant American husband at one of London's most loved churches. I stood on the grand, neo-classical portico looking out through its three-storey columns at Trafalgar Square, dwarfed as she must have been by St. Martin's vast scale. Still, feeling small would have been a pleasure for my giantess who stood seven foot six in her stockinged feet, weighed 413 pounds and tried all her life to exemplify the virtues of a thoughtful Victorian lady.

Although she exhibited with P. T. Barnum in New York during the 1860s, she read widely and dressed in the style of the time, which meant following the fashions in Mr Godey's book for ladies. Her Victorian dresses were so voluminous she is said, on one occasion, to have knocked a man off his chair entering a drawing room. Despite her best efforts, Anna's extraordinary female body remained a challenge to Victorian notions of femininity and a caricature of her own aspirations for respectability.

Both Anna and her groom, Martin Van Buren Bates, were interested in history so it's possible they knew St. Martin-in-the-Fields dates back to 1222 when the monks of Westminster pastured their animals and grew their fruits and vegetables in Covent Garden. But the giants probably chose the cathedral, which was rebuilt in 1722–1724 by the architect James Gibbs, primarily because it was in London's theatre district. It was also close to their new home, an apartment on 45 Craven Street.

The wedding at St. Martin's was an auspicious London event staged with the blessing of Queen Victoria who had asked the couple to appear before her on June 2 at Buckingham Palace. The Queen, who stood only four feet seven inches herself, was so delighted with the pair, sometimes known as the love couple, that she gave Anna a cluster diamond ring and a giant watch and chain to her husband.

The crowd outside St. Martin's after the wedding was so large the police had problems clearing a path for the wedding party as it left for 45 Craven Street. A reporter from London's *Daily Telegraph* politely referred to the groom's panic after he dropped the ring during the ceremony in this way: "A giant may get used to being eight feet, but marrying an eight foot woman while idlers gawk is enough to flummox any old cock. . . "

Whether Anna truly felt satisfied with herself is hard to say. She died in 1888 at the age of 44, worn down by gravity, like most giants, and by the hardship of her last birth labour. But for me St. Martin's remains the place where she stepped so happily into her married life.

SUSAN SWAN
Novelist

1.5 National Portrait Gallery

2 St. Martin's Place WC2, 020 7306 0055

Charing Cross

Particularly now after its brilliant re-planning by Dixon. Jones, the Royal Opera House architects. From the top floor restaurant is my favourite view of the Houses of Parliament; after seeing that I am ready to go back for another look at the sinister Tudor portraits, newly situated in a small, dimly lit gallery which effectively conveys the tense and secretive atmosphere of the era.

LADY STIRLING (AKA MARY SHAND)
Designer

1.6 Gordon's Wine Bar

47 Villiers Street WC2, 020 7930 1408
Embankment, Charing Cross

At the foot of Villier's Street, off the Strand, sits Gordon's, the oldest wine bar in London. A basement entered by neck-breakingly narrow stairs, this fine and squalid place also debouches a few awkward steps on to a shadowy alley where I loll, tumbler of *fino* in hand, with my back to gardens on the Thames embankment. In the summer, live jazz beats the traffic out of the air, and as I look up from the page of a paperback I feel intimately surrounded not only by the 18th century—at an angle I can glimpse Buckingham Street—but by modern business online in glimmering low-level offices, by a country summer breezing over my head and by New Orleans stomping into our metropolis. If you get your moment right (the sherry's always there with its savour of Spain), it's one of not so very many places in London where you have the delicious illusion of the whole world coming your way.

DAVID HUGHES
Writer

I love this place for its triumphant seediness, among so much that is brash and new and smart. The façade is so unassuming that you can pass it without seeing it. Downstairs, half the tables are in candlelit darkness under black, damp arches. The rest of the cellar is hung with prints and posters dating from the 1940s and 1950s. The walls are scabby, the furniture and fittings ancient and I can't think how it's allowed to remain open! It's always buzzing and the wines are excellent.

VICTORIA GLENDINNING
Author and journalist

1.7

The Adelphi

1768–1774, Robert Adam
Strand WC2
Not open to the public.
⊖ Embankment, Charing Cross

Royal Society for the Encouragement of Arts, Manufactures and Commerce (RSA)

1772, Robert Adam
8 John Adam Street WC2, ☎ 020 7930 5115
Not open to the public.
⊖ Charing Cross

Robert Adam's The Adelphi (Greek for the "brothers," that is: Robert, James, John and William) was built between 1768 and 1774, aided by a lottery in 1774. It runs between the Thames and the Strand, and though mutilated in 1936, is a fine statement about Georgian, urban architecture. The grandest is that for the Royal Society of Arts building, by Adam in 1772. His source lay in the quarters of Paris and followed a graduated social structure with the grandest houses in the Royal Terrace (now rebuilt) facing the river, and served as a system of underground streets and passageways—a utilitarian labyrinth that supported, in every sense, the smart society above. Robert and James Adam lived in Royal Terrace from 1773–1778, as did the great actor David Garrick, from 1772–1775. Adam moved in 1776 to the end house beside the river at 9 Robert Street, which survives and is shown in the engraving of the entire scheme of July 1768.

A. A. TAIT
Art historian

1.8 Somerset House

1776

Strand WC2, 020 7438 6622

Temple, Embankment, Charing Cross

Robert Burton gave us a cure for melancholy: "Be not solitary, be not idle." Now we have another one: go to the Fountain Court of Somerset House at dusk.

DUNCAN FALLOWELL
Author

Somerset House now has an elegantly restored cobbled courtyard and new fountains by Dixon.Jones enhancing the architecture. There, the newly installed Gilbert Collection and Hermitage Treasures and, of course, the Courtauld Institute Gallery, are a treasure trove. Walking through the courtyard there is now direct access to Waterloo Bridge with an attractive outside cafe for tea on a warm day and views along and across the Thames.

LADY STIRLING (AKA MARY SHAND)
Designer

1.9 The Royal Opera House

Covent Garden WC2, 020 7304 4000

Covent Garden

Floral Hall

1999, Dixon.Jones

Even if you are not attending a performance in the newly regilded main theatre, go early evening for a drink in the spectacular Floral Hall. Because of political sensitivities and the lottery of funding, architects Jeremy Dixon and Ed Jones almost grew old waiting for their plans for the expansion and refurbishment of the crumbling House to take shape. There is, then, a sense of celebration—and relief—as you take the wonderful extravagant great glass escalator through the vast crystal conservatory. At the top, in a Starck-like bar you can view the early Opera crowd dining below, or take in an unusual sweep of London skyline—including, apparently standing out on the balcony, Nelson on top of his column.

TIM ADAMS
Writer and editor

1.10 Donmar Warehouse

Earlham Street WC2, 020 7369 1732
Covent Garden

The Donmar Warehouse, established by Sam Mendes, is an interesting and unexpected theatrical experience.

SUSAN KLEINBERG
Artist

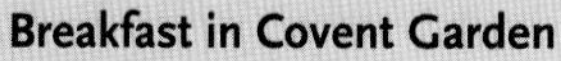

Breakfast in Covent Garden

Covent Garden

1.11 Monmouth Coffee Company

27 Monmouth Street WC2, 020 7379 3516

1.12 Portwine's

24 Earlham Street WC2, 020 7836 2353

My favourite area for shopping early on a Saturday morning is Seven Dials in Covent Garden. The Monmouth Coffee Company sells and serves the best coffee in London while round the corner, Portwine's butcher shop provides the sort of bacon that made Britain great—even if it has been improved by American smoking techniques.

DAVID MILES
Archaeologist

1.13 Denmark Street

Between Charing Cross Road and St. Giles High Street WC2
⊖ Tottenham Court Road, Leicester Square

If rock'n'roll was one of the 20th century's greatest contributions to Western culture, then Denmark Street's place in the grand scheme of history has been criminally underplayed—perhaps because it can hardly claim to be one of London's most respectable thoroughfares. A grubby afterthought of a street attaching its one-way obstinacy to Charing Cross Road's bookish charms, its permanently unswept pavements seem to have the knack of attracting only Soho's more insalubrious denizens. London's Tin Pan Alley it may be but Highway 61 it's not, and The Kinks's "Denmark Street" isn't exactly an ode to be proud of. However, there can't be many streets that the fields of oceanography, contemporary art and rock'n'roll all owe debts to. Only the numerous guitar shops clumsily cranking out a perpetual loop of amateur Led Zeppelin renditions give any clue as to this seedy dog-leg of a street's past.

In the sixties (that Never-Never Land of my parents' youth), the Rolling Stones had their office here, Orange Amplifiers traded off The Who's patronage, and Bob Dylan played the 12 Bar Club—an endearingly shabby folk venue along Denmark Place, a tiny alleyway by Andy's Guitars. In the seventies, David Bowie frequented a long-gone cafe on the south side of the street, Elton John churned out a few hits here and a back room at number 6 gained anti-establishment credibility as the Sex Pistols' rehearsal space.

In the early nineties the street witnessed the nascent twinklings of contemporary British art's global success: Gavin Turk's studio was just round the corner on Charing Cross Road, and squatting broodingly where now sits a respectable copy shop was the infamous Lawren Maben's Milch Gallery. And where would Jacques Cousteau be today without Denmark Street? Augustus Siebe, pioneer of the diving helmet, lived at number 5 at the turn of the 19th century.

From the council tenements that make up Sidney Street to the mess that is Docklands, London's scrappy hotchpotch of post-Blitz architecture belies a history that's as rich in substance as it is hard on the eyes. So next time you marvel at the Mall, or drink in the grandeur of St. Paul's, spare a thought for poor old Denmark Street. Like Janis Joplin, it may not be much to look at, but boy, it's got soul.

DAN FOX
Writer and editor

1.14 Hanway Street

Off Oxford Street north of Soho Square W1
Tottenham Court Road

London can be a hard home: sink or swim, it says. If you're sinking, then the best way to drown is to head for Hanway Street, the side alley that connects the east of Oxford Street to Tottenham Court Road.

Start off in the basement of Bradley's (42–44 Hanway Street, 020 7636 0359) for Guinness, tapas and London's finest jukebox: it boasts the theme tune to *White Horses*, and several Elvis rarities. Your musical appetite piqued, why not sate it with a visit to Division One (36 Hanway Street, 020 7493 5345), a small emporium boasting the finest in old soul and new beats. Return to Bradley's afterwards to eat. (You could try the Hare Krishna restaurant further on, but the food is muck.)

After closing time, Hanway Street opens up. There's Costa Dorada (47–55 Hanway Street, 020 7631 5117), on the right: three quid in on a Friday and Saturday, dogged flamenco dancing, more tapas and room to stretch out and argue. Or there's Pepes (20 Hanway Street), further along the street and down rickety stairs into a den populated with speeding postmen, yabbering artists, loquacious and welcoming late-nighters of all description.

Best of the lot, though, and up in the heavens is Helen of Troy's (22 Hanway Street). Helen, who recently died, was a Soho character in the old sense of the word: she looked after those she liked, and kicked the rest back down the stairs. Charlie has taken on her mantle. You'll have to sweet-talk to get in, but if you're successful you'll find a place where crying is as expected as laughing and no one judges either.

And if you're swimming? Make straight for Oasis (32 Endell Street, ☎ 020 7831 1804), the outdoor swimming pool at the end of Shaftesbury Avenue.

MIRANDA SAWYER
Journalist and television presenter

The French Connection—A Walk Through Soho

⊖ Tottenham Court Road, Leicester Square

1.15 **French Protestant Church**
1893, Aston Webb
8–9 Soho Square W1, ☎ 020 7437 5311

1.16 **House of St. Barnabas**
1 Greek Street W1

1.17 **Manette House**
Manette Street, across from the Goldbeater's Arm W1

1.18 **Kettners**
29 Romilly Street W1, ☎ 020 7437 6437

1.19 **Maison Bertaux**
28 Greek Street W1, ☎ 020 7437 6007

1.20 **Notre Dame de France**
1865, Louis-Auguste Boileau; 1953–1955, rebuilt by Hector O. Corfiato
5 Leicester Place WC2, ☎ 020 7437 9363

Greek Street (named after a Restoration Greek church) was taken over by the French in the 1690s. The influence of those Huguenot refugees still gives the place a French flavour. In the northwest corner of Soho Square is the

French Protestant Church, a deep red Flemish Gothic building designed by Aston Webb who also gave us the façades of the V&A and Buckingham Palace. On the opposite corner at the top of Greek Street stands the House of St. Barnabas, birthplace of the Gothic horror author William Beckford, who received piano lessons from Mozart here. Since 1861 it has been House of Charity for Homeless Women, and is mentioned in Dickens's *A Tale of Two Cities*. Further down Greek Street, if you duck through the arch at the Pillars of Hercules pub, you will enter Manette Street, named in 1895 after Doctor Manette from the same book, and see the house where the Manettes might have lived (the wall opposite it still sports a replica of the Goldbeater's sign described in the novel).

If you're thirsty, nip into Oscar Wilde's favourite restaurant, Kettners (founded in 1868 by Napoleon III's chef), for a quick glass of champagne, or the oldest French patisserie in London, Maison Bertaux (founded by communards in 1871), for a coffee and the best *chocolat religeuse* you will taste outside Paris. Maison Bertaux is run by the eccentric Michele Wade, an actress, who every 14 July performs a *tableau vivante* of the French Revolution in the street outside, complete with a guillotine, *tricolores* and a glimpse of carefully arranged nipple.

Dash across Shaftesbury Avenue, through Chinatown, and into Leicester Place to Notre Dame de France, London's French Catholic church. Built on the grounds of the former panorama, a vast circular oil painting created by Robert Barker in 1793, the building was converted into a church in 1865, much of which was destroyed by bombs during World War II, but was again rebuilt after the war. It still contains Barker's ninety-foot diameter circular plan and inside, there are frescoes painted by Jean Cocteau in 1960.

FIDELIS MORGAN
Writer

1.21 Bar Italia

22 Frith Street W1, 020 7437 4520

Tottenham Court Road, Leicester Square

In an upstairs room at this cafe, John Logie Baird transmitted the first television pictures. Using a mechanical scanner made from a hatbox mounted on a coffin lid, Baird watched as the screen on his "televisor" flickered to reveal the outline of a ventriloquist's dummy (no human had been brave enough to volunteer to be transported across the airwaves); Baird rushed downstairs to tell the world (and Mr Cross, who had an office below). Now, you can sip your espresso, and watch the mixed media executives and film PRs go by.

TIM ADAMS
Writer and editor

1.22 Andrew Edmunds

44 Lexington Street W1, 020 7437 8594

Oxford Circus, Piccadilly Circus

What I liked about Soho when I lived there as a child was its sense of secrecy and history. There are few places in Soho now which still give me this sensation, but one of them is the shop in Lexington Street run by, and called, Andrew Edmunds (who also owns the excellent restaurant of the same name next door). The shop sells 18th-century prints, including English satirical prints, which I have always loved. The building is wonderful too—a panelled Georgian townhouse.

MARK SLADEN
Curator and writer

Air Street

From Glasshouse Street, to cross Regent Street, and ending at Piccadilly W1.

Piccadilly Circus

The weight and mass of the huge stone arches which loom

over the two short halves of Air Street darken the mood, oppress the pedestrian and heighten the drama of emerging into the elegance first of the sweeping curve of Regent Street and then of the pompous parade of Piccadilly.

One of the misconceptions about London is that it lacks grandeur. Walk from the crowded streets of Soho down the vaulted tunnel of Air Street and this misconception will be dispelled. London excels in the juxtaposition of extreme opposites and the contrast between the dirty, dense streets of Soho and the Beaux Arts bombast of the West End is accentuated by this grand alley. The Brobdingnagian scale of the arches, the deep shadows of the rustication and the intense downward pressure of the weighty stone seems to derive from the brooding prison fantasies of Piranesi. The only glimpse of the sky is carefully measured through a colonnade which sits atop the arches creating an unattainable upper level.

Incredibly, the architecture dates from as late as 1923, when Regent Street was rebuilt in its current grand incarnation. Obliquely opposite in Piccadilly you can see one of London's finest storefronts in the Waterstone's store (previously Simpson's), a smooth-faced work of modernism of great clarity which was completed only a little more than a decade after the massive arches of Air Street yet seems to belong to a different world. Air Street acts like a breach in the city walls, a monumental gateway from the genteel world of West End shopping into the dark, Dickensian world of Soho's back streets. Be careful of the piles of black rubbish bags which appear at these city gates during the night, an indication of Air Street's status as the seedy service underbelly of West End grandeur, a stark reminder that this is an unsanitised, if monumental, alley in a big city.

EDWIN HEATHCOTE
Architect and writer

ST. JAMES'S, WESTMINSTER & THE EMBANKMENT

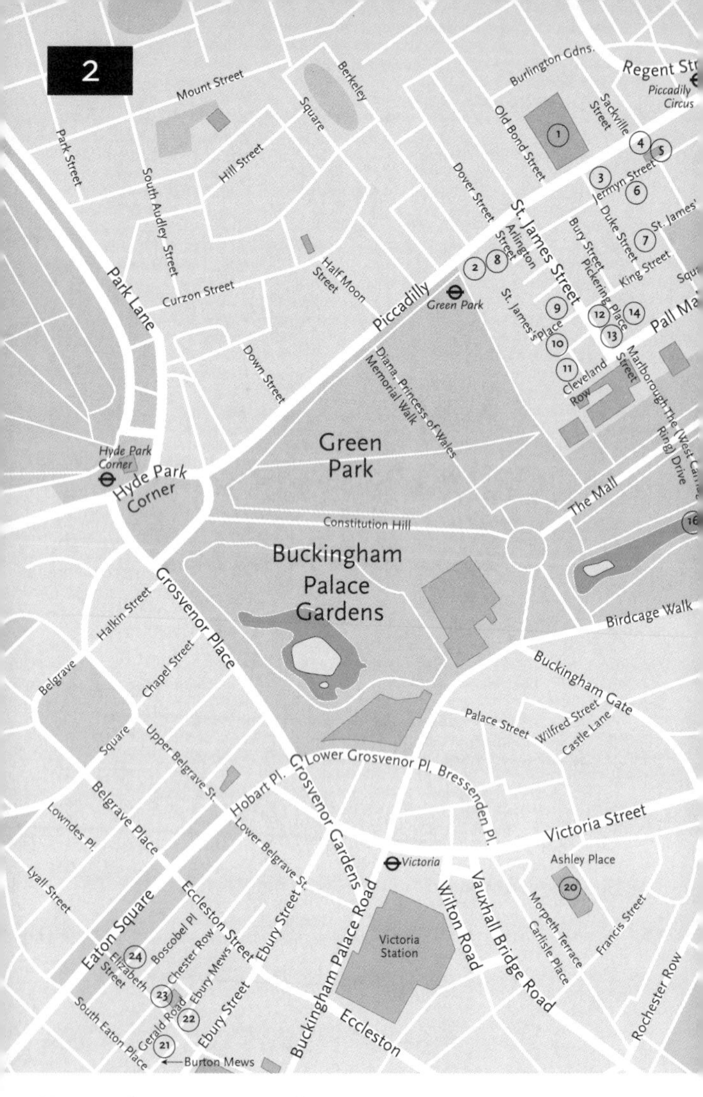

ST. JAMES'S, WESTMINSTER & THE EMBANKMENT

1 The Royal Academy of Arts
2 The Ritz
3 Fortnum & Mason
4 Waterstone's
5 St. James's Church
6 Jermyn Street Shops
7 London Library
8 Wimborne House (see p. 53)
9 Duke's Hotel Bar
10 Spencer House
11 Bridgewater House (see p. 53)
12 The Avenue Restaurant and Bar

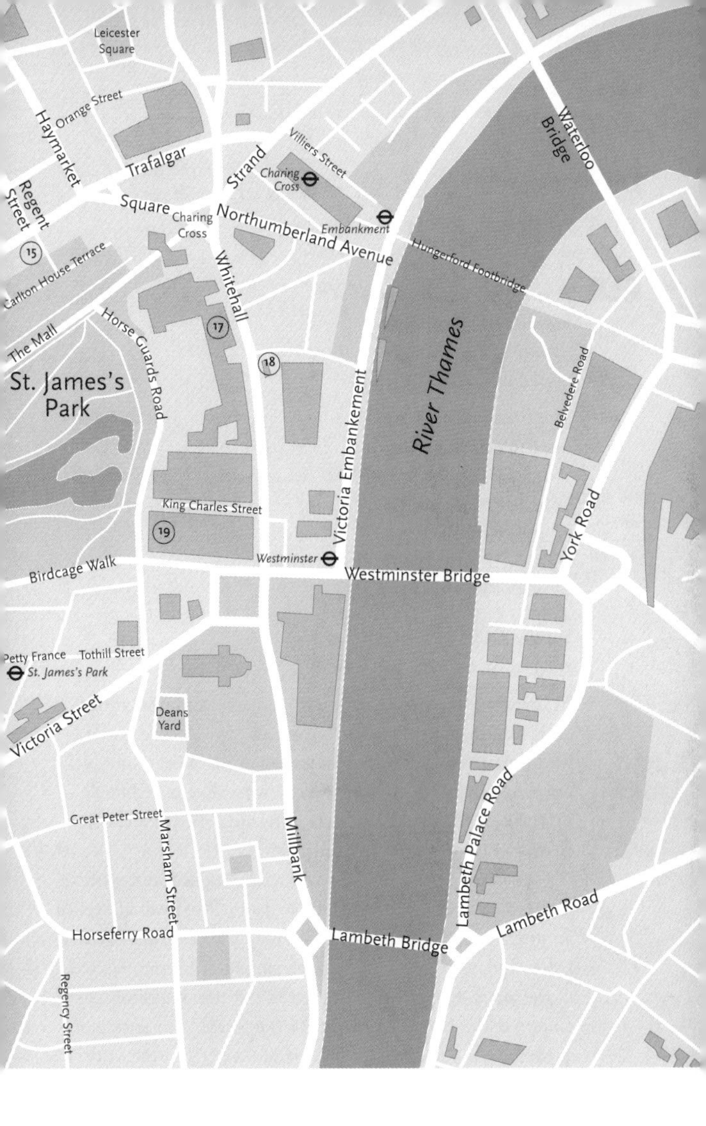

13 Berry Brothers & Rudd Ltd.
14 Pickering Place
15 The Athenaeum Club
16 St. James's Park Lake
17 The Horse Guards
18 Banqueting House
19 Cabinet War Rooms
20 Westminster Cathedral
21 Home of Noël Coward
22 Jeroboam's (see p. 228)
23 Henry Stokes & Co. (see p. 228)
24 Tomtom Ltd. (see p. 228)

ST. JAMES'S, WESTMINSTER & THE EMBANKMENT

2.1 The Royal Academy of Arts

Burlington House
Piccadilly W1, 020 7300 8000
Piccadilly Circus, Green Park

The back of the Royal Academy (used to be the front of the Museum of Mankind). I see its inspiring statues of great thinkers from my office window. David Hume stands opposite Pearson's boardroom, reminding the board of the fallibility of "watertight" principles.

MARJORIE SCARDINO
Chief Executive, Pearson PLC

Sackler Galleries

1989–1991, Foster & Partners

In London, it seems that everyone has an opinion about architecture. Even Prince Charles set off a debate about traditional versus modern styles when he said an unbuilt proposal for the National Gallery was "like a carbuncle on the face of an old and valued friend." Better a carbuncle than needless cosmetic surgery.

The best arguments, however, are in deed, not words, and the best argument for modernism is the lovely jewel of an intervention for the Royal Academy by Norman Foster. Here, a glass stair and a glass elevator have been inserted in the narrow gap formed between the two buildings that comprise the Royal Academy. On one side is the original garden façade of the 1666 house (converted in the 18th century by Lord Burlington) now revealed for the first time in a hundred years, and on the other, the façade of the Victorian galleries. The stair and elevator, beautiful free-standing objects in their own right, lead to a glazed reception hall incorporating the parapet of the original façade. From here one enters the former Diploma galleries which were added above Burlington House in Victorian times. These rooms have been completely renovated, replete with new barrel-vaulted ceilings, and house the changing exhibitions.

This carefully detailed and thoroughly modern upstart manages to simultaneously assert itself while remaining completely respectful of its elders. As a bonus, there is a permanent installation in the glazed atrium of Michelangelo's *Taddei Tondo*. One can only imagine Michelangelo, himself no stranger to breaking the rules, looking down with a smile at being shown here, rather than anywhere else.

ROBERT KAHN
Architect

Tea

2.2 **The Ritz**
1906, Mewes and Davis
55 Piccadilly W1, 020 7493 8181
Green Park

2.3 **Fortnum & Mason**
181 Piccadilly W1, 020 7734 8040
Piccadilly Circus, Green Park

If you long to feel like a member of Britain's royal family, the most proximate equivalent might be tea at The Ritz. Enter the hotel, where the doors are opened by waistcoated men who politely tip their hats. Up the stairs, in the gilded pink and gold tea room, a waiter eyes you for the briefest moment, then seats you at a tiny table and enquires if you require High Tea.

Soon, piled onto your small table, is a three-tiered silver tray. There are triangles of ham, salmon and egg and watercress sandwiches, then a plate full of warm scones, served with clotted cream and strawberry jam, best eaten when the cream and the jam are blended together into a fine pink paste. On the top level of the silver tray, a plate full of coiffed meringues and multi-coloured pastries (which actually look better than they taste) capture the flavour of this beautiful room in which well-dressed men and women contentedly sip and nibble.

An alternative: after shopping for a few small items to take home as gifts at Fortnum & Mason's (pine honey, Major Grey's Mango Chutney, or British Beer Mustard, as well as a plethora of teas and jams), find your way to the Fortnum & Mason tea room in the rear of the store. High tea is served between 3pm and 6pm. The tea itself is not as luxurious, as pretty (nor as costly) as The Ritz, but satisfying in its own right.

Either way, drink plentiful amounts of tea and emerge later into what will almost definitely be a grey and rainy afternoon, to stroll around Green Park.

LEXY BLOOM
Writer and editor

2.3 Fortnum & Mason

181 Piccadilly W1, 020 7734 8040
Piccadilly Circus, Green Park

Soda Fountain

There was a time in my life when I regularly went to the Soda Fountain at Fortnum & Mason. It was redecorated in the 1980s, but retains a rather sugary and slightly kitsch decor that perfectly complements its ice cream sundaes. It has a Rex Whistler-ish look, completely uninfluenced by anything that has ever gone on in architecture schools. The *frisson* produced by a brush with such an interior is the perfect accompaniment to a tall glass of ices, syrups and fruit—there is the same air of innocence and transgressive guilt about both pleasures.

ANDREW BALLANTYNE
Professor of architecture

2.4 Waterstone's

202–206 Piccadilly W1, 020 7851 2400

Piccadilly Circus, Green Park

Studio Lounge Bar

Fifth floor

This is one of the best places in central London for an early evening cocktail (some with absinthe). Pass beyond the exquisite modernist façade into the heart of the old Simpson's department store, grab a pile of books and take the dated lift with its Smarties-coloured buttons to the fifth floor where the bar is on your immediate right. Sit back on a sofa and, between turning pages, enjoy a view which pans from an acute take of the London Eye, through Big Ben, Westminster Cathedral Tower, and out towards the tower blocks of west London. Great at sunset. A tip: if you are able to speed-read your way through a new hardback book you can buy another drink with the money saved.

NICK WYKE

Journalist

2.5 St. James's Church

1676–1684, Christopher Wren

197 Piccadilly W1, 020 7734 4511

Piccadilly Circus, Green Park

Font

End of the 17th century, Grinling Gibbons

Consecrated in 1684, rebuilt after World War II, this is still an elegant space, and an active church with frequent concerts. The charming marble font with a sculpted frieze of Adam and Eve is thought to be a work of Gibbons, who certainly executed the astonishing limewood garlands of flowers, fruit and game. William Blake was christened here, presumably at this font, and curiously enough was later famous for sitting in his garden with his wife, naked, and telling friends that they were playing "Adam and Eve."

JEREMY MUSSON

Editor

RECOMMENDED READING

David Esterly, *Grinling Gibbons and the Art of Carving*, Harry N. Abrams, 1998 (US); V&A Publications, 2000 (UK).

2.6 Jermyn Street Shops

Jermyn Street W1

Piccadilly Circus

The colours and objects in the shop windows in Jermyn Street have remained, over the decades, a feast to behold.

THEODORE RABB

Historian

London Library

Founded in 1841; current building by J. Osborne Smith, 1896–1898.

14 St. James's Square SW1, 020 7930 7705

Green Park, Piccadilly Circus

Club-like lending library with fantastic iron floors, reading room, etc.

GEORGE LOUDON

Chairman, Helix Associates Ltd.

2.9 Duke's Hotel Bar

Hotel built in 1532, architect unknown, then rebuilt in 1885, and remains a Grade II listed building

35 St. James's Place SW1, 020 7491 4840

Green Park

The bar in Duke's Hotel, St. James's, is small, cosy and serves the best martinis in the world. Gilberto, the flamboyant Italian barman, will provide articles from the world's press (*The New York Times*, etc.) to testify to this. Then he brings out a bottle of rare vodka, available nowhere else in Britain and covered with frost, straight from the freezer, plus a glass each, similarly frosted. He pours in a generous measure of vodka and tops it with a swirl of vermouth and a splash of lemon, declaring,

"James Bond was wrong; martinis should not be shaken and should not be stirred." The resulting concoction is rich, creamy, silky smooth and ambrosial. I have enjoyed the best martinis in New York with a Japanese friend who was writing a book on the subject (of martinis). All were pedestrian compared to this. Gilberto is now the star of her book.
LESLEY DOWNER
Writer

2.10 Spencer House

1756
27 St. James's Place SW1, ☎ 020 7499 8620
Open Sundays only; tours must be booked in advance.
⊖ Green Park

An enjoyable short walk across Green Park will lead you to Spencer House, one of the rarest survivors of the grand noble houses commissioned by the great families of the 18th century. The house in St. James's Place is still owned by the family of the late Diana, Princess of Wales and recently has been impeccably and lovingly restored by Lord Rothschild. A must for those interested in the most sophisticated aristocratic taste of the mid-18th century and the results of restoration at the highest level.

The house was originally built between 1756–1766 by the first Earl and Countess Spencer, after they had eloped at his coming of age party; the Spencers uncompromisingly employed the best craftsmen and architects of their day. Designed for lavish entertaining, the house contains some of the most perfect and earliest neo-classical interiors and furniture in England hidden behind its impressive façade. The magnificent parade of ground-floor rooms, still used during the week, culminates in the stunning green and gilded Palm Room designed by John Vardy whilst upstairs the series of glittering salons by James "Athenian" Stuart command fine views of the park.
JEREMY GARFIELD-DAVIES
Antiques dealer

London's Horses

In 1900, London streets were jammed with omnibuses, hansoms, vans, wagons and growlers—all pulled by some of the 300,000 horses that lived and worked in the city. A century later the horses have disappeared except for a few used by the police, the army on ceremonial occasions, and riders in Hyde Park. But their past importance is reflected in an enormous number of equestrian statues in London. Do not expect historical or anatomical accuracy. Opposite Big Ben a pair of over-large fiery animals threaten to overturn the rebellious British Queen Boadiccea (or more accurately Boudicca) in her exotic, oriental and historically inaccurate chariot (Thomas Thornycroft, 1850s). Does any other city have a statue to someone who destroyed it? On the other side of Parliament, by St. Margaret Street, Richard the Lionheart—one of England's more useless kings—is magnificently mounted on a spirited charger (Carlo Marochetti, 1861), a contrast to Field Marshall Earl Haigh's wooden rocking horse (Alfred Hardiman, 1937) on Whitehall or Edward VII's apparently drunken mount at Waterloo Place (Bertram Mackennal, 1922).

In Trafalgar Square, dominated by Nelson's column and traffic, it is easy to overlook the superb little equestrian statue of Charles I by Herbert Le Sueur (1633). Like so many of its breed, it was influenced by the Marcus Aurelius prototype in Rome. And tucked anonymously away, at the junction of Piccadilly and Dover Street, is perhaps the finest equestrian statue, the mythical horse and rider by Elizabeth Frink (1974).

And the horse that beat them all? Whistlejacket, whose portrait by George Stubbs (1762), hangs in the National Gallery.

DAVID MILES
Archaeologist

2.12 The Avenue Restaurant and Bar

7 St. James's Street SW1, 020 7321 2111

Green Park

Rick Mather's exciting essay in spacey urban chic, ultra-modern but perfectly at home in a traditional part of town, and fit for a Martian duke. Just to walk past it at night is to be involved in strange theatre, or some kind of installation, playing to the street yet aloof from it. The food is pretty good, too.

DUNCAN FALLOWELL
Author

2.13 Berry Brothers & Rudd Ltd.

est. 1698

3 St. James's Street SW1, 020 7396 9600

Green Park

The most gracious shopping experience in London without doubt is a visit to Berry Brothers & Rudd, wine and spirit merchants to the Queen and the Prince of Wales, who have carried on business at their sublime lopsided premises since the 17th century. There is no finer place to buy a bottle of claret than in this unchanging shop with its creaking uncovered floorboards, collection of ancient bottles, large set of beam-scales and the courteous service of yesteryear.

PETER HORROCKS
Barrister

Famed for selling and sourcing the best wines, particularly claret, Berry Brothers gives equal attention to a highly rare case of Château Latour as a single bottle of their famed Cutty Sark whisky. Behind the green-shuttered façade the Victorian clerks' desks stand on the ancient undulating floor whilst on the scattered Georgian chairs clients quietly discuss their next purchase with the highly knowledgeable staff.

A huge old coffee scale on which most of fashionable London has been weighed since the 18th century still hangs in the shop beside framed telegrams that include one gravely reporting the loss of a consignment of wine aboard the *Titanic*. Once their clients may have included Napoleon, countless European monarchs and famous figures, but now they could equally include pop stars and shrewd dot.com millionaires.

Below the shop lie the cavernous cellars, rumoured to link with St. James's Palace by a lost tunnel, which now also play host to dinners and tastings for both private and corporate clients. Berry Brothers has moved with the times and now sports arguably the best wine web site around as well as opening a recent presence at Heathrow Airport in case that delicious vintage is still too much of a temptation on the way back home.

JEREMY GARFIELD-DAVIES
Antiques dealer

2.14 Pickering Place

Behind 7 St. James's Street SW1

Green Park

I love the sequence of spaces, materials, surfaces and textures in this short detour in the walk from Pall Mall to Piccadilly. As you go up St. James's Street, pass the Georgian shopfront of Berry Brothers (see above); follow its gnarled paintwork through a little alley that opens up into a microcosm of Georgian townscape. Only about twelve metres square, paved in stone, and surrounded on three sides by four-storey brick buildings—with a sundial at its centre—there it is. No one would let you build it now—not enough light, too much overlooking—but it works. A charming outdoor room. Then back to St. James's Street, and up the hill, and past more organic paintwork on the hat shop. A magical experience.

EDWARD BURD
Architect

2.15 The Athenaeum Club

1830

107 Pall Mall SW1, 020 7930 4843

Charing Cross

F. E. Smith, later the first Earl of Birkenhead, used to pause here every day on his way home from the House of Commons, to urinate. After some months the porter asked if he were a member.

"Member?" the Earl said. "Do you mean this is a club, as well?"

BRIAN MASTERS
Author

2.16 St. James's Park Lake

St. James's Park SW1

St. James's Park

After a long day visiting museums, my favorite place to unwind is by the lake in St. James's Park. The many beautiful and unusual aquatic birds offer a visual delight—especially for a New Yorker like me who is used to Central Park's pigeons. The lake offers not only great bird-watching but also wonderful people-watching as a broad cross section of tourists and Londoners walk by.

NADINE ORENSTEIN
Curator

Bridge over the lake

1957, Eric Bedford. Built to replace the original suspension bridge, which dated to 1857 and was built by Rendell and Co.

Stand in the middle of the footbridge that crosses St. James's Park Lake and look east at the prospect away from Buckingham Palace. Rising up beyond the water crowded with ducks, swans and herons and fringed by weeping willows are the grey turrets, minarets and rooftops of a cluster of imposing white buildings. These are various offices of the Government that line Whitehall, but the view is strikingly un-British. I always imagine it to be a vast Tsar's palace in St. Petersburg, or a snapshot of Disneyland. It's a magical and romantic vista, crowned by the upper half of the London Eye.

NICK WYKE
Journalist

Late at night, with the light from the gas lamps, preferably rain, quiet and with extraordinary views, this is one of the most romantic sites in London.

RICK HAYTHORNTHWAITE AND JANEEN HAYTHORNTHWAITE
Company director and art historian, respectively

2.17 The Horse Guards

1751, William Kent and John Vardy
Whitehall SW1
Charing Cross, Embankment, Westminster

The west front indicates the grandeur of the place, but the centre block court on the east illustrates its refinement. It takes time for the eyes to adjust. What are those projections over the side arches? Hogarth published a cartoon of the royal coachman having his head knocked off passing under the "too small" centre arch. However, it is really part of a careful proportioning system. While you are there, you should visit the Banqueting House by Inigo Jones next door (see below).

ROBERT LIVESEY
Architect

2.18 Banqueting House

1622, Inigo Jones
Whitehall SW1, 020 7839 8919
Charing Cross, Embankment, Westminster

The most important and most unassuming building in Whitehall is Inigo Jones's Banqueting House. A building externally hard to distinguish from the cold façades of government ministries, but in reality one of the hidden delights of Westminster. The interior is, at first sight, indigestible but it contains the fabulous ceiling by Rubens and the perfect Palladian proportions of Inigo Jones. Passed daily by thousands of tourists, a slice of genius is available inside for a mere £3.60.

SIMON THURLEY
Director, Museum of London

Westminster Walk

⊖ Westminster

The tranquil backstreets of Westminster (Barton, Cowley and Lord North Street) are lined with splendid Georgian houses, built for artisans, that have grown crooked with age. The original street signs are engraved in stone tablets and dated 1722. If you look closely, a fading arrow and the letter "S" can be seen on the ground-level façade of some of the houses, indicating the underground World War II bomb shelters. At the end of Lord North Street looms the rare Baroque grandeur of St. John's in Smith Square. Discovering these beautifully preserved streets—most of which are still residential—is made all the more exciting by their being just a stone's throw from such tourist standards as Westminster Abbey and the Houses of Parliament.

NICK WYKE
Journalist

2.19 Cabinet War Rooms

Clive Steps
King Charles Street SW1, ☎ 020 7930 6961
⊖ Westminster

In a corner of Horse Guards Parade opposite St. James's Park, you can walk through a small door surrounded by sandbags into the underground warren of rooms from which the British Government ran the war when Hitler was dropping bombs on London.

Nowhere is more evocative of the old world in which the fortunes of war were tracked by coloured pins on faded maps. The pins are still there, stuck forever onto what was left of Europe when the lights were turned out on them for the last time, and the door was locked, three months after VE Day.

Thirty-five years later it was reopened to the public. Years that had seen the liquidation of the British Empire had left magically unscathed the rooms from which Churchill had fought to preserve it. The typing pool, the dormitories, the cabinet room, Churchill's own bedroom—everything breathes the tobacco-stained, down-at-heel heroism of our finest hour.

NICHOLAS HYTNER
Director

Architecture by Underground

In December 1999, the Jubilee Line extension, which links the Docklands and Greenwich to central London, officially opened. Costing approximately £3.2 billion, the completed line includes platform edge glass doors, eleven new stations, and 59 new trains. (See also p. 76.)

Get on the Jubilee Line at Westminster. Get off at all the stations, one by one, along the route to North Greenwich. View the latest work by many of the stars of modern British architecture—Hopkins, MacCormac, Jiricna, Foster. The greatest spectacle is at Canary Wharf, where Norman Foster's station, 313 meters in length, ellipsoid in its plan, admits radiant shafts of light deep into the station cavity. Escalators soar heavenward. Is this the nearest we now get to viewing a Gothic cathedral for the first time?

FIONA MACCARTHY
Biographer and critic

RECOMMENDED READING

Kenneth Powell, *The Jubilee Line Extension*, Lawrence King, 2000.

2.20 Westminster Cathedral

1892–1903, John Francis Bentley

Ashley Place SW1, 020 7798 9055

Victoria, Westminster

It is the work John Francis Bentley, his master work. The Cathedral contains the exquisite reliefs of the fourteen Stations of the Cross by English sculptor Eric Gill, the anarchist typographer.

AL ORENSANZ

Director, Angel Orensanz Foundation

2.21 Home of Noël Coward

1930–1956

17 Gerald Road SW1

Sloane Square

Having moved across the street from grimy Pimlico, the century's quintessential Englishman and, by 1931, the highest earning author in the Western world, left his mother's boarding house for the whitened sepulchres of Belgravia. Number 17 Gerald Road was hidden away in a mews house and former artists' studio, complete with a gallery and miniature stage on which The Master could perform in private. Sadly there is now no public access but you can still look on from the outside and imagine the parties that defined high society: princes of the realm and transatlantic superstars rubbed elbows over cocktails and laughter, whilst Coward himself kept half an ear open for dialogue which would find its way into his latest play. "It was," commented a contemporary edition of *Vogue*, "a party in the enlightened tradition, all very white and witty." Coward would spend the next morning prising tonic bottle caps out of the carpet.

PHILIP HOARE

Writer, curator and presenter

RECOMMENDED READING

Philip Hoare, *Noël Coward*, Simon & Schuster, 1996 (US); Random House, 1996 (UK).

HYDE PARK & CHELSEA

3
Moscow Road
Bayswater
Lancaster Terrace
Lancaster Gate
Queensway
Lancaster
Gate
6
Bayswater Road
North Walk
Notting
Hill Gate
Kensington Gardens
Lancaster Walk
The Long Water
The
Round
Pond
Kensington Church Street
Palace Gardens Terrace
Kensington Palace Gardens
7
8
9
5
Serpentine Road
York House
Place
Holland Street
Kensington
Church Walk
10
11
12
Kensington High Street
Kensington Gore
Kensington Road
De Vere
Gardens
Palace Gate
13
Victoria Road
Kensington
Square
High Street
Kensington
Exhibition Road
Queen's Gate
Gloucester Road
Abingdon Villas
Scarsdale Villas
Lexham Villas
20
Brompton Rd.
Cromwell Road
Cromwell Road
15
Queensbury
Place
Gloucester Road
18
Thurloe Street
14
Harrington Rd.
Bute St.
19
Pelham Street
South
Kensington
Stanhope Gdns.
Harrington Gdns.
17
16
Onslow
Square
Sumner Place
Earl's
Court
Earl's Court Road
Cranley Place
Onslow Gdns.
Ixworth Pl.
Old Brompton Road
Sydney Street
Cale Street
Roland Gdns.
Warwick Rd.
The
Boltons
Drayton Gdns.
Dovehouse Street
Old Brompton Road
Redcliffe Gardens
Coleherne Road
Fulham Road
Finborough Road
West Brompton
Hollywood Road
29
Park Walk
Elm Park Rd.
Oakley Street
Brompton
Cemetary
Seagrave Road
Old Church Walk
Upper
Cheyne Row
Cheyne
Row
Cheyne
27
Cheyne Walk
Beaufort Street
Edith Grove
King's Road
Gunter Grove
Cheyne Walk
Battersea
Bridge
Fulham Road
Fulham Broadway

HYDE PARK & CHELSEA

1 Hyde Park Corner
2 The Grenadier
3 Egg Contemporary Crafts and Clothing (see p. 110)
4 Sunday Softball
5 Serpentine Gallery
6 Kensington Gardens
7 Kensington Palace Gardens
8 The Orangery
9 Kensington Palace
10 Kensington Church Walk
11 St. Mary Abbots Church
12 Former house of Ezra Pound
13 Former house of Henry James
14 Daquise Restaurant
15 The Institut Français
16 Christie's
17 La Bouchée
18 La Grande Bouchée
19 The French Bookshop
20 The Victoria & Albert Museum
21 Cadogan Square and Lennox Gardens
22 Chelsea Royal Hospital
23 Stable Block
24 Oscar Wilde's House
25 Ziani's
26 Chelsea Physic Garden
27 Carlyle's House
28 The Albert Bridge
29 Fulham News (see p. 228)

HYDE PARK & CHELSEA

3.1 Hyde Park Corner

Intersection of Knightsbridge, Grosvenor Place, Piccadilly and Park Lane, in between Hyde Park and Green Park

⊖ Hyde Park Corner

Hyde Park Corner is a frantic traffic roundabout bordered by Apsley House (Wellington's old home, with the enviable address: number 1, London); Knightsbridge, the Lanesborough Hotel; the walls to Buckingham Palace Gardens; Green Park; Piccadilly; and Park Lane. Subways from all corners lead to this fascinating oasis.

Here stands Decimus Burton's Constitution Arch, once the entrance to Hyde Park. Now it is marooned and unused, except by royalty; I once witnessed Princess Margaret being driven through it to queue-jump the snarl of traffic. The Arch is topped with a magnificent bronze group: *Peace in her Quadriga*, by Captain Adrian Jones. Captain Jones gave a dinner party for eight friends inside the statue before it was raised to its present position. In the base of the Arch there is a tiny police station—the second smallest in London (the smallest is in Trafalgar Square).

Unquestionably the sexiest naked back in London (best viewed in a car coming out of Park Lane) belongs to the bronze David, part of Frances Derwent Wood's Machine Gun Corps Memorial. David leans on Goliath's sword; wreathed machine guns stand either side of him and the statue bears the chilling motto: "Saul hath slain his thousands, but David his tens of thousands."

Opposite the Lanesborough is The Royal Artillery Memorial (by Charles Sargeant Jagger). It takes the form of a huge field gun guarded by eloquent bronze gunners, and is inscribed to "a royal fellowship of death." It is positioned so that if a shell were fired from it with sufficient propulsion it would land on the Battlefield of the Somme.

FIDELIS MORGAN
Writer

3.2 The Grenadier

18 Wilton Row SW1, 020 7235 3074

Hyde Park Corner

Near the end of a cobbled mews cul-de-sac in London's most exclusive neighbourhood, Belgravia, is a delightful pub, The Grenadier. A huge Victorian gas lamp, sentry box and flower baskets adorn the outside of the pub, where steps lead up to a snug room with a four-hundred-year-old pockmarked chrome bar. Hidden away—even cab drivers have problems finding this one—some believe the pub is haunted by the eponymous soldier who is said to have been flogged to death by fellow card players after being found cheating. The pub claims to make London's best Bloody Mary and was recently visited by Madonna and entourage for post-concert drinks. There's even a cosy restaurant at the back of the pub, serving tasty but quite expensive fare.

NICK WYKE
Journalist

3.4 Sunday Softball

Hyde Park SW7

Knightsbridge

Every Sunday morning, from April to October, a group of expatriate Americans gathers in Hyde Park, opposite the Knightsbridge Barracks, to play softball. This game has been going for forty years; I've played in it both with my father, in the 1960s, and my sons, in the 1990s. The park is a good place to visit on Sunday mornings, before the museums and galleries open, and if you know how to play, you might even get a game.

On many Sundays red-coated guardsman parade past the field, accompanied by a band, and play stops briefly, as it does when a child or a dog wanders into left field, which happens a lot. On other occasions, like Remembrance

Sunday, immaculate ex-guardsmen file past in bowler hats, pin-striped suits, carrying tightly furled umbrellas, a uniform all but extinct elsewhere in Britain, even in the City. Then the pubs open (and there are several quiet, attractive ones in the little streets and squares between the park and Harrod's). If you've spent any time at the game—watching, playing, kibitzing—and feel tourist guilt, walk west a few hundred yards and you're at the Serpentine Gallery or the Albert Memorial, newly gleaming after its interminable restoration.

ZACHARY LEADER
Professor of English literature

3.5 Serpentine Gallery

1912, Sir Henry Tanner
Kensington Gardens W8, 020 7402 6075
Lancaster Gate, South Kensington

Go to the Serpentine Gallery (free) in Kensington Gardens and then watch the roller-bladers, baseballers and the rest as you pay respects to Prince Albert, who now boasts the most splendid memorial in town.

GILLIAN DARLEY
Architectural writer

The Serpentine Gallery combined with a walk in the park towards The Orangery in Kensington Gardens.

ALEXANDRA SHULMAN
Editor

3.6 Kensington Gardens

Lancaster Gate, South Kensington, Queensway, High Street Kensington

Kensington Gardens, with its tremendous avenues, its splendidly bombastic statuary (I except the obnoxious Peter Pan) and its two sheets of water is the most beautiful of the city's famous parks. Walk southward from Lancaster Gate under the majestic plane trees (best in winter—black tracery against London's mother-of-pearl sky). Bear left for a visit to the Serpentine Gallery—good one-person shows of contemporary art—then meander northwestward through the artfully wooded wilderness (avoid the goose-shit-spattered shores of the Round Pond) to Hawksmoor's Orangery (see p. 54), now a restaurant where you can eat lunch for an inordinate price but in unsurpassable grandeur.

LUCY HUGHES-HALLETT
Writer

High Society

High Street Kensington, Notting Hill Gate SW1

2.10 **Spencer House**
27 St. James's Place

2.8 **Wimborne House**
22 Arlington Street

2.11 **Bridgewater House**
Cleveland Row

3.7 **Kensington Palace Gardens**

No other European city so cynically destroys its historic architecture. Even so, the widespread demolition of Georgian Mayfair in the course of the 20th century is a mystery which still causes pain. The noblest mansions of Piccadilly and Park Lane, of Grosvenor Square and Berkeley Square, were pulled down within living memory in a ghastly alliance of British philistinism and commerce. Spencer House is the finest and best-known survivor, but ask Eagle Star Insurance company (020 7495 5563) if you can look at Wimborne House (though they demolished the sensational belle epoque ballroom). The post-Georgian Bridgewater House, Barry's huge stone *palazzo* overlooking the Green Park, survives as the most secretive great home in London—what does go on there? But the sublime atmosphere of pre-1914 *richesse* can now really

only be found in one London street, Kensington Palace Gardens, a late arrival to the society map, put up in the middle of the 19th century, adjacent to Kensington Palace. This uninterrupted flow of magnificence in mature gardens exerts a quiet and very potent grandeur.
DUNCAN FALLOWELL
Author

3.8 The Orangery

1704–1705, Nicholas Hawksmoor (under Christopher Wren)
Kensington Gardens W8, ☎ 020 7938 1406

On a rainy London day (or fine day), spring, summer, or fall, take a walk in Hyde Park to Kensington Gardens. Have lunch or tea in the Orangery's high-ceilinged, airy space. Simple stone floor, black iron tables and chairs, crisp white tablecloths (and luscious pastries!). Sit at a table along the back wall to get a long view into the manicured gardens out front. Better yet, stop beforehand at Notting Hill Books (132 Palace Gardens Terrace, W8, ☎ 020 7727 5988). Find a book on something one knows nothing about: Land Tenure of the Ramessides, or the History of Notting Hill, even a new bestseller, all of which will be discounted. Read in the Orangery—no one is rushed. Go around two in the afternoon, when lunch is winding down and tea has not yet started. Afterwards, continue reading by the Round Pond nearby, sitting on a deckchair provided by the Royal Parks Service. As swans glide and children play, I have my London.
CECILIA WONG
Interior designer

RECOMMENDED READING

Kerry Downes, *Hawksmoor*, Thames and Hudson, 1969.
Roger White, *Nicholas Hawksmoor and the Re-planning of Oxford*, Exhibition Catalogue, British Architectural Library Drawings Collection, Ashmolean Museum, Oxford, 1997.

3.9

Kensington Palace

1689–1727

Kensington Gardens w8, 020 7937 9561

High Street Kensington, Queensway

An alternative approach: having admired the south front of Kensington Palace from Kensington Road, turn right into Kensington Church Street and second right into York House Place. This leads to Kensington Palace Green and opposite lies the original 18th-century entrance to the palace. A footpath leads past the security gates, used by the various members of the royal family who live in the palace, and through a side gate into the park. Walk around Wren and Hawksmoor's south front of 1689–1695 and the neo-Palladian east elevation of ca. 1718, thought to be by Colen Campbell and built between the earlier pavilions of Nottingham House, to the public entrance beyond the Sunken Garden: a charming detour. Once inside, remember to look out from the state apartments, remodelled by William Kent in 1722–1727, from which Charles Bridgemen's garden design of about the same date is still evident in the radiating avenues.

ANNE PURCHAS

Architectural historian

William Kent Architecture

Lancaster Gate, South Kensington

3.9

Cupola Room

Kensington Palace, Kensington Gardens w8, 020 7937 9561

High Street Kensington, Queensway

2.17

Horse Guards

Whitehall sw1

In 1722 William Kent, wit, dilettante and darling of Lord Burlington's Palladian clique, launched his London career with the *grisaille* decoration of the Cupola Room at

Kensington Palace. At the Horse Guards in Whitehall, (see p. 42), his last project in 1755 (where you can view the Changing of the Guard) he has become "Kentissimo." Remarkably, you can still walk from one to the other entirely through the Royal Parks, a distance of some two and a half miles through central London, and a delightful way to pass a summer's afternoon.
PETER HOWARD
Architect

3.10 Kensington Church Walk

Off Kensington High Street W8
High Street Kensington

Take a turn up this small alley, whose entrance is by the side of the Old Kensington Town Hall. Quite suddenly you are in a quiet York stone walkway and church yard which continues further to a small row of single storey shops with a pretty forecourt. There are benches to sit on, bird song, antiques and antiquarian books. Perfect for a quiet respite.
RALPH STEADMAN
Artist

3.11 St. Mary Abbots Church

1868–1872, Sir George Gilbert Scott
Kensington High Street W8, 020 7937 5136
High Street Kensington

A lunchtime concert at St. Mary Abbots Church on the corner of Kensington High Street and Kensington Church Street, with its peaceful cloister, is an uplifting experience. Here students from the Royal College of Music will transport one into another world (and coffee is available before the performances, which start at 1pm on most Fridays).
ANNE PURCHAS
Architectural historian

Literary Neighbours

High Street Kensington, Gloucester Road w8

3.12 **Former house of Ezra Pound**
10 Church Walk

3.13 **Former house of Henry James**
34 De Vere Gardens

Not long after arriving in London, Ezra Pound moved into 10 Church Walk, Kensington (1909–1914). You are likely to be regarded with suspicion by the residents as you stand in the tiny square gazing upwards at the second-floor window where Pound worked on the translation of *Cathay*, and brushed up *Lustra* for publication.

One day not long ago I went to make an imaginative claim on Henry James's house at 34 De Vere Gardens (where, unlike Pound's House, there is a blue plaque), where he lived between 1886 and 1902, overseeing, among much else, the publication of his great London novel, *The Princess Casamassima*. I was tickled to discover that it was just a short hop away from Pound's place. But surely there was no connection between these two expatriate Americans, one grounded in the 19th century, the other an architect of the 20th? Then, flicking through a biography of Pound in the library a few days later, I came across the information that when he arrived in London and moved into Church Walk, he had a dislike of fiction, "of which, anyway, he was ignorant, apart from the novels of Henry James."

JAMES CAMPBELL
Writer and editor

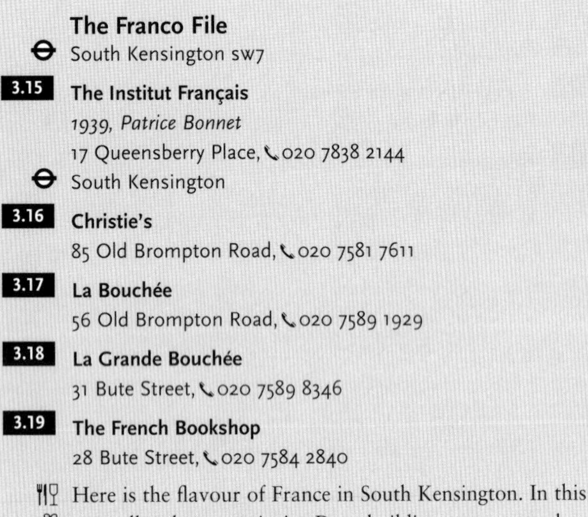

The Franco File

South Kensington SW7

3.15 **The Institut Français**
1939, Patrice Bonnet
17 Queensberry Place, 020 7838 2144
South Kensington

3.16 **Christie's**
85 Old Brompton Road, 020 7581 7611

3.17 **La Bouchée**
56 Old Brompton Road, 020 7589 1929

3.18 **La Grande Bouchée**
31 Bute Street, 020 7589 8346

3.19 **The French Bookshop**
28 Bute Street, 020 7584 2840

Here is the flavour of France in South Kensington. In this marvellously eccentric Art Deco building you can read *Le Figaro* over an espresso or lunch in the *brasserie*, explore the multimedia library, see a film in the cinema, perhaps one of the great classics by René Clair or preview one of the newest offerings. There might even be a wine tasting or a lecture.

The nearby Old Brompton Road is a real cosmopolitan hub, avoiding the crowds and razzmatazz of the King's Road. Here you can visit Christie's to view the next sale, which might be pictures, furniture, or Pop memorabilia, sit at a pavement table for coffee, and get a proper French meal at La Bouchée. Or, go around the corner to Bute Street for your Camembert and Brie from La Grande Bouchée or the latest novel from Paris at The French Bookshop.

MICHAEL BARKER
Designer, author and publisher

3.14 Daquise Restaurant

20 Thurloe Street SW7, ☎ 020 7584 4944
South Kensington

Next to South Kensington tube, just round the corner from Exhibition Road and all the museums, hides this plot of Poland in Central London. Grubby steamed up windows obscure a warm, old fashioned—and wonderfully reasonable—haunt of the Polish *émigré* community and those in the know. A shot of vodka on a cold day with herrings followed by some *golubtsy* (stuffed cabbage) served with all the chaos of family-run kitchens is the perfect antidote to the pretensions of imperial London outside. In summer, an Eastern European cream cake and coffee.

If you are lucky, you might still catch a table of military looking gents on their daily trip from the Polish Club in Hammersmith to the Polish Hearth Club for the evening: some airmen who fought in the Battle of Britain, some victims of unspeakable atrocities in Germany or Russia, others simply *émigrés* who, history has determined, spend their lives in a foreign land. And London unknowingly feeds off them and their children—another wave of enriching immigrants.

ANGUS MACQUEEN
Documentary film-maker

3.20 The Victoria & Albert Museum

Cromwell Road SW7, ☎ 020 7938 8500 or 020 7938 8441
South Kensington

The V&A has got pictures up to the ceiling; it's like hanging out in my grandmother's attic.

MARJORIE SCARDINO
Chief Executive, Pearson PLC

The Pirelli Garden

The garden was opened in 1987 and designed by Cecil Denny Highton. The surrounding buildings date from 1856–1882 and were designed by Francis Fowke and Henry Scott.

On a hot summer's day, the Pirelli Garden in the courtyard of the Victoria & Albert Museum is as pleasant a place to be as any in London. Tucked away in a corner on the south side are two small ceramic plaques that record past companions: "In Memory of Jim, Died 1879, Aged 15 Years. Faithful Dog of Sir Henry Cole, of this Museum" and "To TYCHO A faithful dog who died V IAN MDCCCLXXXV."

Cole (1808–1882) was not just "of this museum," he in fact created it, as the South Kensington Museum (its name was changed to the V&A in 1899). Cole was one of those multitalented indefatigable Victorians, a public servant whose achievements included developing the Penny Post, creating the modern Public Record Office and masterminding the Great Exhibition of 1851. If this makes him sound impossibly worthy, these memorials reveal a more human side, and it is reassuring that creating one of the world's great museums did not make Cole so self-important that he was unable to commemorate the dog who can, indeed, be seen by his side in photographs of the buildings under construction.

In a way the memorial to Jim works better as a memorial to Cole himself than the unsatisfactory portrait of Cole to be found on the Ceramic Staircase in the southwest corner of the courtyard, and is in much the same spirit as that archetypal piece of Victorian sentimentality, Sir Edwin Landseer's painting *The Old Shepherd's Chief Mourner*, displayed in the Henry Cole Wing of the V&A.

JAMES BETTLEY
Architectural historian

RECOMMENDED READING

John Physick, *The Victoria and Albert Museum: The History of Its Building*, V&A Publications, 1982. o.p.

3.21 Cadogan Square and Lennox Gardens

Knightsbridge SW1

⊖ Knightsbridge, Sloane Square

Cadogan Square and Lennox Gardens in Knightsbridge are lined with late 19th-century buildings (Grade II listed) with exquisite details. They were in part designed by George Devey. Stroll through in the evening to glean glimpses inside of the many beautiful stucco ceilings and grandiose entrance lobbies.

GABRIELE BRAMANTE
Architect

Chelsea Sunday Morning

⊖ Sloane Square

3.22 Chelsea Royal Hospital
1689–1692, Christopher Wren
Royal Hospital Road, ☎ 020 7730 0161
Mass is at 11am on Sundays; arrive before then for entry

3.23 Stable Block
The Royal Hospital
1814–1817, Sir John Soane

3.24 Oscar Wilde's House
44 Tite Street

3.25 Ziani's
45–47 Radnor Walk, ☎ 020 7352 2698

At 10:30am walk or drive (park inside) through the front gate of Sir Christopher Wren's Chelsea Royal Hospital, on the Royal Hospital Road. Walk through to the Parade ground and enjoy the banter of the pensioners as they assemble for parade in their scarlet tunics, black tricorn hats, and white gloves. Watch the Sergeant Major barking his orders and the Governor arriving to inspect the parade.

After the short parade, walk into the Wren chapel for matins; the congregation face each other across a central nave. For the British, the experience is a slice of old Britain; for overseas visitors it is quite baffling, but unforgettable. After the service, if you know a pensioner, don't miss the chance of a pint in the mess and if you don't, wander all the same past the mess to the western end, for a glimpse of the stables designed by Sir John Soane.

Finish the morning by walking up Tite Street past the house (number 44) where Oscar Wilde lived, through Tedworth Square into Radnor Walk for a wonderful lunch at Ziani's, one of London's best and most friendly Italian restaurants tucked away on this side street off the King's Road.

CHARLES MARSDEN-SMEDLEY
Designer

3.23

Stable Block

1814–1817, Sir John Soane

The Royal Hospital, Royal Hospital Road SW3

Sloane Square

As with jewels, splendour in architecture does not depend on size. On the south side of Royal Hospital Road in Chelsea stands a small but veritable "gem" created by one of England's greatest architects: Sir John Soane (1753–1837). The surviving Soane public buildings in the capital are familiar landmarks and are all much visited, including Dulwich Picture Gallery (see p. 231), Pitshanger Manor Museum in Ealing and Sir John Soane's Museum (see p. 116) in Lincoln's Inn Fields. The Chelsea Stable Block is widely acknowledged by aficionados as being one of his finest exteriors, yet it remains little known to the general public.

The front (northeast) elevation is an architectural masterpiece in terms of abstract composition. With its concentric brick arches and "layering" of planes of meticulously constructed brickwork, it exemplifies Soane's minimalist primitive style. The underlying geometry of the design is clear for all to see, and detailing and ornament are reduced to a minimum. Note the elemental cornice of brick triglyphs and the highly idiosyncratic chimneystacks. For Soane, even horses deserved fine buildings to live in!

BARRY CLAYTON
Architect

RECOMMENDED READING

Dorothy Stroud, *Sir John Soane, Architect*, Studio Books, 1961.
Gillian Darley, *John Soane: An Accidental Romantic*, Yale University Press, 1999.
Margaret Richardson and Mary Anne Stevens, eds., *John Soane, Architect: Master of Space and Light*, Royal Academy of Arts, London, distributed by Yale University Press, 1999.

3.26 Chelsea Physic Garden

66 Royal Hospital Road SW3, ☎ 020 7352 5646
Open Wednesdays and Sundays from April to October.
Entrance on Swan Walk

 Sloane Square

London's most secret garden is the Chelsea Physic Garden, only unlocked to the public on Wednesday and Sunday afternoons between early April and late October. Catch it open if you can for its historical interest and its extraordinary melancholy beauty. Make your way there via Sir Christopher Wren's 17th-century Chelsea Royal Hospital (see p. 61), a cosier English equivalent of the Hôtel des Invalides in Paris, inhabited by frail but still roguish scarlet coated pensioners. Think Byronic thoughts of mutability as you contemplate Wren's Chapel and Hall hung with tattered banners of ancient campaigns.

FIONA MACCARTHY
Biographer and critic

3.27 Carlyle's House

24 Cheyne Row SW3, ☎ 020 7352 7087

 Sloane Square

Take a bus or the Circle/District line to Sloane Square on

a Wednesday morning. Visit Thomas Carlyle's house, wonderfully preserved and little visited. Climb up to his (semi) sound-proofed study and feel glad that you didn't have to cook in the meagre kitchens down below. Lunch at one of the pubs round the corner and go into Chelsea Old Church before spending a leisurely afternoon at the Physic Garden (see p. 63), five minutes' walk away. It is open every Wednesday and Sunday and has jolly guides on hand, if you wish for them.
MIRANDA SEYMOUR
Biographer, novelist and critic

River Walk

To walk along the Thames Embankment, past Chelsea Old Church, Cheyne Walk, and the Chelsea Royal Hospital (see p. 61), preferably on an autumn evening at the hour favoured by Whistler (a nearby resident), with leaves from the giant plane trees—stirred up by passing traffic—blowing around your legs as you look out over the broad sweep of water, is to experience a moving poetic loneliness within the warmth of the population of a great city.
JAMES DUNNETT
Architect

3.28 The Albert Bridge

1873, designed by Roland Mason Ordish; modified in 1890 by Joseph Bazalgette
Between Chelsea and Battersea Park SW3 and SW11
 Sloane Square

It's an absolutely beautiful 19th-century structure, like a cat's cradle made out of steel. It has a sign on it telling marching men to break step at the bridge—which seems to have been news to more recent bridge builders.
MARJORIE SCARDINO
Chief Executive, Pearson PLC

OXFORD STREET & MAYFAIR

OXFORD STREET & MAYFAIR

1 Royal Institute of British Architects
2 The Victoria
3 The Wallace Collection
4 BBC Broadcasting House
5 A Walk Along Oxford Street
6 Middlesex Hospital Chapel
7 Brazilian Touch Cafe
8 Hat Factory
9 Claridge's Hotel
10 Michaeljohn

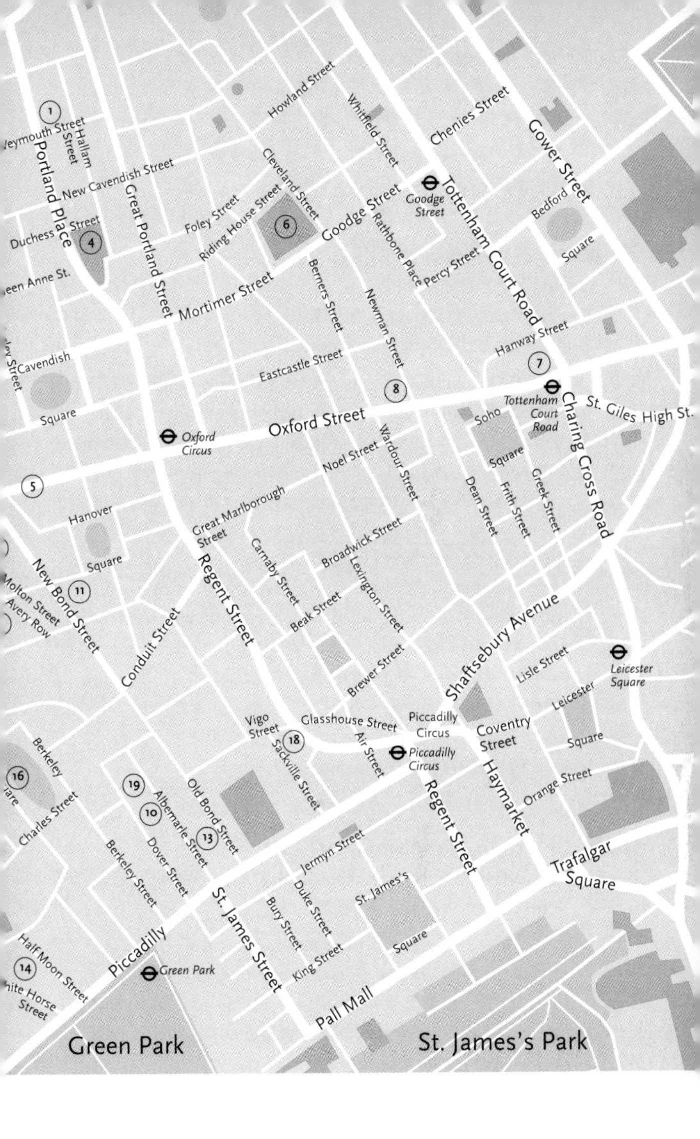

- 🎁 11 Fenwick
- 🎁 12 Browns
- 🎁 13 Charbonnel et Walker
- 🍴🍷 🎁 14 Shepherd Market
- 15 Crockfords
- 16 The Clermont Club
- 17 Farm Street Church / Church of the Immaculate Conception
- 18 Austin Reed Store
- 19 The Royal Institution

OXFORD STREET & MAYFAIR

4.1 Royal Institute of British Architects

1932–1934, Grey Wornum

66 Portland Place W1, ☎ 020 7580 5533

⊖ Regent's Park, Great Portland Street

The RIBA is a classic example of a thirties building commissioned by architects for architects. Its architect, Grey Wornum, a progressive traditionalist, won the job in open competition in 1932. The symmetrical simplicity of its exterior belies an astonishing openness inside: do walk up to the second floor and look down at the imaginative handling of the staircases and the transparency of the glass screens. The quality and craftsmanship of its applied decoration and sculpture, all of which symbolises architecture and the building trades, make it the most interesting piece of art of the inter-war period in London.

MARGARET RICHARDSON
Curator

RECOMMENDED READING
Margaret Richardson, *66 Portland Place*, RIBA Publications, 1984.

4.3 The Wallace Collection

Hertford House, Manchester Square W1, ☎ 020 7935 0687

⊖ Bond Street

The Wallace Collection has the reputation of being a repository of *l'ancien régime* at its most self-indulgent. Indeed it is crammed with Sèvres and Boulle and ormolu, the dimpled flesh of Boucher and the costly gleam of Titian and Velázquez and Rembrandt, lovely Watteaus, a remarkable collection from the golden age of Dutch painting and choice offerings in more specialised fields, armour, majolica and mid-19th-century French academic art. All housed in Lord Hertford's and Sir Richard Wallace's skilfully refurbished mansion, offering now a tranquil covered courtyard. Happily (or sadly!) you will not find crowds. This is

London's Frick Collection. When will there be concerts in the courtyard on Sundays?
PETER CARSON
Publishing editor and translator from Russian

If you want a refuge from the maelstrom of Oxford Street, walk north past Selfridge's and across Manchester Square to the Wallace Collection. There you will be delighted by the delicate paintings of Boucher and Fragonard and the rather less delicate portrait of *The Laughing Cavalier*, splendidly displayed in a historic house full of 18th-century French furniture. In the courtyard, now roofed over to provide a light and spacious restaurant, you can meet friends or lunch over a newspaper.
DAME JENNIFER JENKINS
President, Ancient Monuments Society

This is one of the best collections in London and very few ever go. You can sit in an almost empty room and enjoy Titians and Rembrandts (only one is now recognised, though many were before) in peace. It's also known for 18th-century French painting. Recently extended.
RON GRAY
Author

4.4 BBC Broadcasting House

1932, G. Val Myers
Portland Place W1, 020 8743 8000
Regent's Park, Oxford Circus

A temple to Lord Reith's aspirations for the BBC. It's curved like a great ship, the prow facing into London. But it reminds me of something else as well. In the 1560s, the Flemish painter Pieter Bruegel the Elder did two paintings of the Tower of Babel, a structure weirdly like Broadcasting House. According to Genesis, God prevented the completion of the tower by causing everyone to speak in mutually incomprehensible languages. This seems very apt for the "babel" of voices which have emanated from

the BBC over the years. Once you've seen the similarity, you can't forget it. And it's a marvellous building.
VICTORIA GLENDINNING
Author and journalist

4.5

A Walk Along Oxford Street

Between Marble Arch and Tottenham Court Road WC1
Marble Arch, Tottenham Court Road

Plans drawn up in 1972 to transform Oxford Street into "a tree-lined paradise" must have fallen down the back of somebody's sofa, because the busiest street in Britain can still, on occasion, make you lose the will to live—mainly at Christmas, when bright-eyed shoppers (Gap! Boots! Foot Locker!) spill out of the ground at Oxford Circus and congeal in a fog of bus fumes and freshly roasted caramel nuts, £1, while the Metropolitan police attempt crowd control with loudhailers.

Still, pleasure and pain have always been what Oxford Street does best. Nineteen-year-old Thomas De Quincey bought his first dose of opium here one rainy autumn Sunday in 1804 and never forgave the "stony-hearted stepmother" of a place. This is a Roman road; the sun sets at the Selfridge's end and bounces off Centrepoint, near to which condemned prisoners from Newgate got tanked up before the final mile of their lives, west along to Tyburn gallows by Marble Arch. Little club-footed Lord Byron was born at 24 Holles Street, now the John Lewis Department Store. Look up here and you'll see a Barbara Hepworth sculpture she made in 1962, an attempt to give a sense of moving "in air and water." She lived in St. Ives, though, not WC1.

In its day, Oxford Street was more than just a cheap Rolex watch. The Salvation Army at Regent Hall, number 275, occupies the site of an old ice rink; Oxford Walk shopping precinct the site of the 1840s Princess's Theatre, where world-famous tenors competed in decibels. Masquerades drew beautiful people to the Pantheon, with its stunning rotunda modelled on Santa Sophia in Constantinople; it opened in 1772 at number 173 and burnt down twenty years later. Marks and Spencers stands in its place today and though the exotic may now only be seen in terms of an M&S microwave-able chicken tikka masala for one, there is still a kind of unmissable cosmopolitan quality here. These days though it's left to a Greek-Cypriot fiddle player outside Debenham's to put on a bit of a show. Nick Leonidas, blinded by yellow fever as a child, has busked here since 1981: five days a week, 52 weeks a year, 11am to 7pm with a half-hour break at three.

CAROL MCDAID
Journalist

4.6 Middlesex Hospital Chapel

J. L. Pearson, 1890–1891
Mortimer Street W1, 020 7387 9300
Goodge Street, Oxford Circus

A real gem, actively and poignantly in use by patients, visitors and staff. Nikolaus Pevsner admires its "sumptuously ornamented marble and mosaic."

PATRICK MORREAU
Consulting engineer

4.7 Brazilian Touch Cafe

40 Oxford Street W1, 020 7636 7222
Tottenham Court Road

Through the back of Oxford Street's 24-hour Whistlestop Supermarket is a tiny corner of Brazil, where they serve deliciously authentic *feijoada* (pig parts with black beans, the Brazilian national dish) accompanied by the sounds of Brazil.

LUCINDA MONTEFIORE
Radio producer

4.8

Hat Factory

105 Oxford Street W1

Tottenham Court Road, Oxford Circus

Maddening to cross the traffic of Oxford Street at any time, but if you are stuck outside the HMV shop or nearby, walk with your back to the Marble Arch end, to Newman Street which crosses Oxford Street to become Great Chapel Street on the south side. The block on this corner was built in 1887 as a hat factory for Henry Heath, whose name is majestically lettered on the workers' entrance round the back, on Hollen Street. At 105 Oxford Street, the central facia is decorated by four carved figures associated with the hat trade. Designed by Benjamin Creswick, a protégé of Ruskin, they are visible high against the skyline, and include a delightful stone beaver, contemplating a jump down onto the roof, or wagging its paddle in disapproval when observed by a tipsy eye.

GEOFFREY ELBORN
Writer

4.9

Claridge's Hotel Bar

55 Brook Street W1, 020 7629 8860

Bond Street

Walk to Old Bond Street, familiar from smash and grab movies, to buy stiletto boots from Gina Shoes (9 Old Bond Street, 020 7409 7090). Have a chocolate martini in Claridge's Bar. If I were meeting God for a cocktail, I'd take him to this Art Deco paradise.

CAROLE MORIN
Novelist

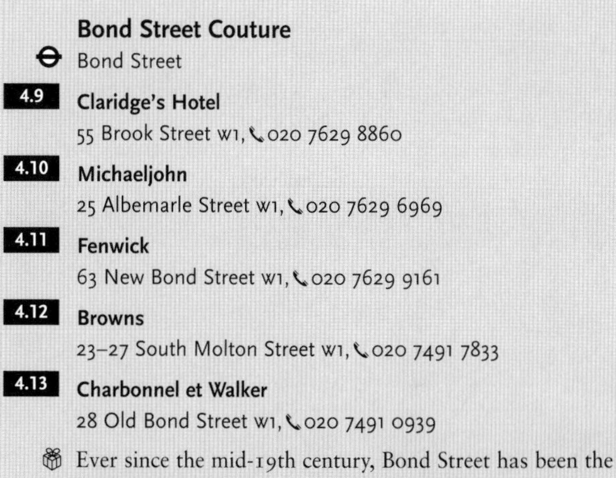

Bond Street Couture

Bond Street

4.9 **Claridge's Hotel**
55 Brook Street W1, 020 7629 8860

4.10 **Michaeljohn**
25 Albemarle Street W1, 020 7629 6969

4.11 **Fenwick**
63 New Bond Street W1, 020 7629 9161

4.12 **Browns**
23–27 South Molton Street W1, 020 7491 7833

4.13 **Charbonnel et Walker**
28 Old Bond Street W1, 020 7491 0939

Ever since the mid-19th century, Bond Street has been the epicentre of fashionable shopping. Beau Brummell took regular strolls here, so that smart society could admire his clothes. Now the typical Bond Street shopper is more likely to check in at Claridge's Hotel nearby, and wend her perfumed way to Michaeljohn on Albemarle Street, where she'll have a haircut or a spa treatment before submitting to the strain of purchasing that Versace dress or Cartier ring.

You don't have to be quite so at home here, though, to admire the view. On the main drag, big name fashion houses jostle for position: Prada, Hermès, Donna Karan, Armani, Calvin Klein, Nicole Farhi, Louis Vuitton. In general, the more recent the arrival, the larger the shop. But this competitive scene is not all there is. Bond Street has tributaries that open out onto other worlds. Savile Row is still the home of royally appointed tailors, and a new guard, of brighter shirts and hipper suits, have set up shop across the street. The arcades (Royal Arcade off Bond Street and Burlington Arcade off Burlington Street) have the hushed, old-world charm of 19th-century Paris, while Cork Street, a few paces to the East, is lined with galleries, and forms the heart of the contemporary art world.

At the north end of Bond Street is Fenwick, a department store slightly more modest than Harvey Nichols, and opposite it, a few yards down Brook Street, is the mouth of South Molton Street. South Molton Street, famous for Browns, the cutting-edge clothing emporium that can make or break a young designer's career, is also the handiest place to stop for coffee. But if you happen to find yourself at the Piccadilly end of Bond Street, choose a few chocolates from Charbonnel et Walker, and eat them while gazing into the windows of Tiffany's next door. Breakfast has never been better.

GABY WOOD
Writer

4.14 Shepherd Market

Turn on to Half Moon Street from Piccadilly, which leads to Shepherd Market W1

Green Park

Shepherd Market is bounded by Piccadilly and Curzon Street. I first saw it during World War II, when available ladies patrolled its streets, keeping up the raffish tradition of the 18th-century May Fair (which gave its name to the surrounding area). Both the May Fair and the ladies are gone now, although, in the early 1950s, when I took my wife there for the first time, she remarked, "Isn't it interesting that the dress shops have their models walking back and forth outside in front of them." Today, there are a variety of ethnic restaurants, pubs and small shops; it's good for a snack or a meal almost any time of day or night.

KENNETH SEEMAN GINIGER
Publisher

RECOMMENDED READING

H. V. Morton, *In Search of London*, Methuen Publishing Ltd., 1988, o.p.

Gambling

Gaming Board for Great Britain, ☎ 020 7262 6200

1.24 **Golden Nugget**
22 Shaftesbury Avenue W1, ☎ 020 7439 0099

4.2 **The Victoria**
150-162 Edgware Road W2, ☎ 020 7262 7777

6.17 **Ladbrokes Casino**
61-66 Russell Square WC1, ☎ 020 7833 1881

4.16 **The Clermont Club**
44 Berkeley Square W1, ☎ 020 7493 5587

4.15 **Crockfords**
30 Curzon Street W1, ☎ 020 7493 7771

As a semi-compulsive gambler I'd point you in the direction of London's numerous casinos. In the West End you've got the Golden Nugget, which is a bit shabby and full of waiters from Chinatown gambling between shifts. Dress code here is "smart casual," which means no jeans, trainers or shorts. Pretty much anything else is acceptable.

If you're a poker player there are two casinos: The Victoria on Edgware Road, which has a fairly large card room that hosts small games where you can sit down with £50, all the way up to the big game which will cost you £500 for starters. For a friendly game and some cheap entry competitions try the Ladbrokes Casino on Russell Square. At both these you'll need a jacket on—the definition of jacket tends to vary, but lapels are a good idea.

If you're a high roller you probably know about The Clermont and Crockfords already. But if you fancy losing money in splendid comfort, I'd recommend these two. Both are in Mayfair.

In London, the kindly Gaming Board wants to protect you from yourself, so you can't just walk into a casino and play, you have to be a member (or a guest of a member). So you'll have to plan ahead by 24 hours. Good luck.

PATRICK MARBER
Playwright

Underground Design

The London Underground is a must for an architectural detective. As London is built on clay it was possible to burrow and connect every corner of the city and suburbs. There are 19th- and 20th-century survivals everywhere with arcaded embankments, cast iron columns, wooden platform canopies and furniture, glass and metal light fittings.

At Baker Street, the Edwardian panelling is as good as in an ocean liner. At Aldgate East, there are embossed creamware 1950s tiles; at Covent Garden glazed brick arches the colour of toffee and canary yellow bands. They are della Robbia blue at Knightsbridge. Arnos Grove has a complete 1930s station. Piccadilly Circus another, opened in 1928, and circular. Hammersmith is almost completely 1950s. At Tottenham Court Road there are mosaic murals by Eduardo Paolozzi (1984) and at Canary Wharf Norman Foster's beautiful new station (2000). And everywhere there is Edward Johnston's sans serif lettering, the red white and blue symbol, and the coloured map which is both a work of art and very clear. Nearly everything needs cleaning and mending, of course, but don't be put off by that. . .

DAVID MLINARIC
Interior designer and decorator

4.17 Farm Street Church / Church of the Immaculate Conception

114 Mount Street W1, ☎ 020 7493 7811
⊖ Bond Street

This is the Jesuit church where Graham Greene frequently confessed adultery. Despite its association with famous Catholic converts, the ornate church contains a mysterious spiritual silence alongside its glamour. Popular for Sunday mass with Mayfair diplomats, it is usually empty on weekdays. Light a candle, then eat coconut ice cream in the adjoining Mount Street gardens.

CAROLE MORIN
Novelist

4.18 **Austin Reed Store**

103 Regent Street W1, 020 7734 6789

Piccadilly Circus

Joseph Emberton Barber Shop

1930s

The chrome and marble interior of this Art Deco barber shop has an austere glamour that is given a frivolous edge by an extraordinary twisting light fixture. It looks like the set of a Hollywood musical, and has survived remarkably intact, tucked away in the basement. Emberton was also responsible for Simpson's Piccadilly (now Waterstone's), and the HMV building on Oxford Street, as well as the exhibition buildings at Olympia and the Casino building on Blackpool Pleasure Beach—and the Royal Corinthian Yacht Club, which was featured in the first edition (but not the second) of *The International Style* (H. R. Hitchock and P. Johnson).

ANDREW BALLANTYNE
Professor of architecture

RECOMMENDED READING
Henry Russell Hitchcock and Philip Johnson, *The International Style*, reissue, W.W. Norton and Co., 1997.

Edgware Road

Edgware Road runs northwest from Marble Arch to St. John's Wood Road

Marble Arch, Edgware Road

For me, one of London's strongest features is how it can become somewhere else entirely. Nowhere is this more true than the stretch of the Edgware Road between Marble Arch and the Marylebone flyover, once darkness has fallen. The pavement is suddenly dominated by grizzled, and always friendly, Arabs, strategically arranged over at least two chairs each, deftly sucking on giant shisha pipes containing

apple or strawberry tobacco. Combined with the eerie glow of the lights, it is one of the most interesting nights spent abroad in London.
SHEZ 360
Artist

The Royal Institution

21 Albemarle Street W1, 020 7409 2992
Green Park

Faraday Museum
1813

A compact museum of Faraday memorabilia. In the 19th century, Michael Faraday was a pioneer of the uses of electricity. Here in the museum you will find the world's first electric motor (the springboard of the transport industry), the world's first induction ring (the basis of the world's power supply) and the very first sample of benzene to be isolated (and hence the basis of the world's chemical industry). There is nowhere else in London where so much of technological importance has sprung from such a small area.
P. W. ATKINS
Professor of chemistry

REGENT'S PARK & CAMDEN TOWN

REGENT'S PARK & CAMDEN TOWN

1 Gasometers
2 Lodging House
3 A Stroll in Regent's Park
4 Open Air Theatre
5 St. John's Lodge
6 London Zoo
7 Primrose Hill
8 Lemonia

9 Odette's
10 Primrose Hill Books
11 Cachao
12 R. J. Welsh
13 Abbey Road Studios
14 Lord's Cricket Ground
15 The Shaker Shop
16 Ravi Shankar Restaurant

REGENT'S PARK & CAMDEN TOWN

5.1 Gasometers

Goods Way near Pancras Road NW1

King's Cross/St. Pancras

For proof that structures can be wonderfully poetic, make for the area just north of St. Pancras Station to see an extra ordinary cluster of 19th-century cast-iron gasometers—seven in all. They are visible at a distance from the footpath by the Regent's Canal, or can be inspected at close hand in Goods Way. Best of all, though, take a local train out of St. Pancras, and as it slowly emerges from the station the gasometers—skeletal and cylindrical—will perform an intricate ballet for you, shifting, coiling and criss-crossing.

ANDREW MEAD

Architectural writer

RECOMMENDED READING

Ian Nairn, *Nairn's London*, Penguin UK, 1966 (UK), o.p. Later reissued with a new commentary: *Nairn's London: The Classic Guidebook*, revisited by Peter Gasson, Penguin, 1988.

5.2 Lodging House

8 Royal College Street (formerly Great College Street) NW1

Camden Town

The house at 8 Great College Street (now Royal College Street), where Rimbaud and Verlaine stayed in 1873, is marvellously grubby and dilapidated. It was a foul lodging house then, and looks as if it's something of the same now. It should be the subject of a preservation order in its present state.

JAMES CAMPBELL

Writer and editor

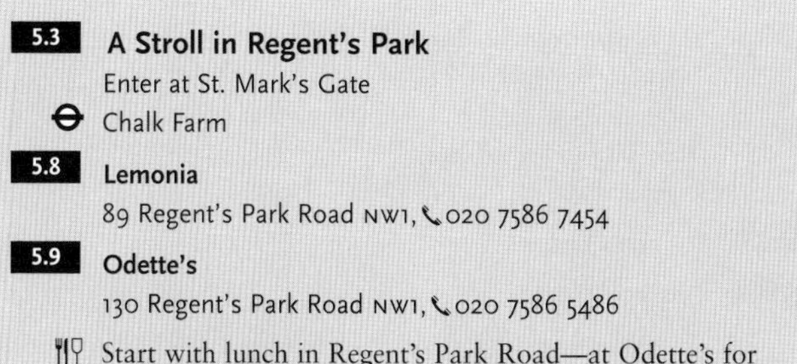

5.3 **A Stroll in Regent's Park**
Enter at St. Mark's Gate
Chalk Farm

5.8 **Lemonia**
89 Regent's Park Road NW1, 020 7586 7454

5.9 **Odette's**
130 Regent's Park Road NW1, 020 7586 5486

Start with lunch in Regent's Park Road—at Odette's for French treats in a room of mirrors, or Lemonia for Greek delights in a noisy bustle. Then limber up by crossing nearby Primrose Hill and enter the park by St. Mark's Gate, bowling along the Broad Walk with the Zoo to the right. All of this area in London's most beautiful park has been lately renovated and improved, climaxing in the sensational Italian Gardens abutting the Euston Road—a formal oasis of bushes, flower beds, small trees, fountains and hedges—restored in the original Victorian design. Regent's Park is an ever-changing landscape of treasures and pleasures. One nook I particularly like is near the Open Air Theatre (see below), an idyllic, enclosed corner with a magnificent Triton fountain, the muscular merman blowing away on his conch with naked bronze ladies revelling in the spume at his fin.

MICHAEL COVENEY
Theatre critic

5.4 **Open Air Theatre**
Regent's Park NW1

Go to the Open Air Theatre, which was carefully smartened up recently, then to the lake; hire a boat and row aimlessly around the island for an hour. After that you should catch newlyweds being photographed in the flashiest part of the gardens, or just sit and sniff roses in Queen Mary's gardens.

GILLIAN DARLEY
Architectural writer

High Summer in Regent's Park

Inner Circle, Regent's Park NW1, 020 7935 5756 or 020 7486 1933
Open May to September
Regent's Park

5.5 **St. John's Lodge**

5.4 **Open Air Theatre**

Go to the Regent's Park when you want to be outside but it's too hot to walk. Take a picnic to the formal garden adjoining the east side of St. John's Lodge. It's a supremely civilised composition of topiary and rosy arbours, stone fountains and velvet lawns, and mercifully few people even know it's there. Afterwards make your way across Queen Mary's rose garden, feeding your scraps to the ducks, to the Open Air Theatre. Always (weather permitting) the most attractive theatre in London, it is also currently putting on a run of first-rate productions. See anything Shakespearean directed by Rachel Kavanaugh, whose sense of comedy is so sure she managed to make even Peter Quince's base mechanicals funny.

LUCY HUGHES-HALLETT
Writer

5.6 London Zoo

Regent's Park NW1, 020 7722 3333
Regent's Park

Penguin Pool
1933, Berthold Lubetkin

An icon of modern architecture, the space is at once a constructivist sculpture, minimalist building and structural delight.

ROBERT LIVESEY
Architect

5.7 **Primrose Hill**
Between Regent's Park and Camden Town NW3
Chalk Farm, Swiss Cottage

5.8 **Lemonia**
89 Regent's Park Road, 020 7586 7454

5.10 **Primrose Hill Books**
134 Regent's Park Road, 020 7586 2022

5.11 **Cachao**
144 Regent's Park Road, 020 7483 4422

5.12 **R. J. Welsh**
156 Regent's Park Road, 020 7722 5113

Primrose Hill is a good place for a refreshing walk, and provides a splendid view of London. It is just to the north of the Zoo, separated from Regent's Park by the Regent's Park Canal, and is less than ten minutes' walk from the Swiss Cottage underground station on the one hand and Chalk Farm underground on the other. There was once a sort of altar on its summit (nothing to do with the Druids who congregate there to celebrate the summer solstice), engraved with a diagram of the view identifying its main features, chief among them the dome of St. Paul's. But the view has become so complicated (the dome is still visible but dwarfed by many tall buildings) that the "altar" has been removed. Many of the park's great trees have gone, too, swept away by the "hurricane" of 1978; but their successors are growing on well, and there is plenty of green shade in which to have green thoughts. Pre-AIDS, this little park led a double life: by day a haven for children's picnics, gentle groups of baseball players, and dog walkers; after dark, a well-known romantic trysting place for gays. But now owls and the occasional fox have the nights more or less to themselves.

At the foot of the hill, to the left if you are facing the Zoo, is short, pretty Regent's Park Road. It is well supplied with shops both useful and elegant, and boasts more than its fair share of excellent cafes—for the shameless sweet-tooth I must recommend the American-style pancakes at Cachao. It also has a lovely Greek restaurant, Lemonia; a famous old-fashioned hardware shop, R. J. Welsh; and arguably the best small bookshop in London (both new and second-hand books), Primrose Hill Books. Locals have been heard to claim that you could manage perfectly well without ever setting foot outside this, their friendly and civilized "village."

DIANA ATHILL
Retired publisher

Climb the 206 feet to the top of Primrose Hill and see London lying at your feet. Where people now fly kites, duels were once fought. Almost two centuries ago, in 1821, the editor of *Blackwood's Magazine* inflicted a mortal wound on the editor of the *London Magazine* for accusing him of being so ungentlemanly as to make money out of his writing. Nearer our own times, Pongo in *101 Dalmations* started the twilight barking from the top of the Hill. Zigzag down between the trees Frank Auerbach paints with such vibrancy (one or two of those paintings are in the Tate Modern) towards the elegant sweep of the Snowdon aviary in London Zoo. Cross the road into Regent's Park taking an almost hidden path to the right down to Regent's Canal. As you stroll along the towpath you get a free glimpse of various beasts behind bars to your left as well as an occasional elephant taking the air. If you look carefully along the wall on the right you can still see the rope marks left by the horses pulling barges—you may even see Britain's oldest narrowboat being drawn by Queenie and Bonny.

EVA TUCKER
Novelist and short story writer

I am by temperament a South Londoner, having been born there. But I seem to have settled (for nearly thirty years now) in northwest London. Not fashionable and expensive Hampstead, but Belsize Park, which shares the NW3 postal district number with Hampstead, but lacks some of its pretentiousness. My nearest open space is Primrose Hill, and I like it partly because it's one of the most inaccessible open spaces in London. I suggest approaching Primrose Hill on foot through the long Victorian and Edwardian streets in the area, permanently in a condition of decay cut short just in time by refurbishment. Look out for blue plaques, depending on your route—Frederick Delius (44 Belsize Park Gardens NW3), Sylvia Plath (3 Chalcot Square NW1), and the socialist historian H. N. Brailsford (37 Belsize Park Gardens NW3), are among those I pass regularly.

By any route, walk to the top of Primrose Hill, a bare unadorned area of short but not aggressively trim grass fringed by trees—on a clear day, this is the best vantage point in North London for seeing how the city has grown and developed, and dignified itself with fine buildings and spoilt itself with deplorable ones.

ALAN BROWNJOHN
Poet

Cruising to Camden Market

Little Venice to Camden Town by barge, along the Grand Union Canal. Generally, trips run every day from April until around Christmas, and then, until spring, only on weekends; phone ahead for hours.

British Waterways, ☎ 020 7286 6101; or London Waterbus Company, ☎ 020 7482 2550; or Jason's Canal Trips, ☎ 020 7286 3428.

⊖ Warwick Avenue for Little Venice; Camden Town for Camden Town

To journey by the canal is to see a place from an entirely different perspective and this short trip, about twenty minutes, is no exception. It starts in Little Venice with its respectable, fashionable villas and houseboats; dives into a tunnel, comes up briefly for air in an estate of low-cost housing; back under a bridge and immediately you are among millionaire mansions on the edge of Regent's Park. Beyond them is the tranquillity of the park in a deep cutting with overhanging trees. The canal bisects the London Zoo; we saw gazelles and heard the squawk of tropical birds. Just after the Zoo, the barge takes a sharp left turn by a floating Chinese restaurant before arriving in Camden.

The barge drops you right at the centre of the Camden market. The day we went there was a cloudless sky with bright sharp sunlight so that the arrival at the crowded market, with is bright colours and exotic smells, owed more to a Conrad arrival at some riverside town on the Congo, rather than a north London market.

CHARLES MARSDEN-SMEDLEY
Designer

5.13 Abbey Road Studios

3 Abbey Road NW8, 020 7266 7000
St. John's Wood

There are certain religious pilgrimages that all music fans (teenage and grown) must undertake. Fans of Jim Morrison visit Père-Lachaise in Paris; fans of Elvis trek to Graceland. And in London, Beatles fans go to Abbey Road to see the legendary studio where the Beatles spent seven years recording.

Take the tube to St. John's Wood, where a five-minute walk leads down Grove End Road to the corner of Abbey Road. You know you are there when you start to see graffiti on the wooden benches lining the road: "Niels Tiebosch loves Beatles;" "Julie + James, 9/11/00, Love is all you need." Then you hit that famous sign: Abbey Road NW8. The zebra crossing, instantly recognizable, is just past the street sign. Close your eyes and picture John, Ringo,

Paul and George parading across. Don't, though, try to pose for a photo: it's actually a very busy intersection full of motorists annoyed by camera-happy tourists.

Abbey Road Studios, at number 3 Abbey Road, is a part of EMI. Skyrocketed into fame because of the Beatles, it has actually been in existence since 1927, when Captain Osmund "Ozzy" Williams decided to build a recording studio in North London. In the 1930s, Sir Edward Elgar conducted the London Symphony in *Land of Hope and Glory*, and in the 1940s, Glenn Miller recorded there. It wasn't until 6 June 1962 that the Beatles made their first visit to the studio (with Pete Best instead of Ringo) and the first song that the Beatles (as we know them) recorded there the next year was "Love Me Do," in Studio 2. The *Abbey Road* LP, the Beatles' tenth and final album to be recorded, was released 26 September 1969. The photo of Paul on the crossing, shoeless, led to rumours that he was really dead.

Today, an average day brings at least thirty fans to Abbey Road, where the outside wall of studios is covered in graffitied writings. They are in English, Spanish, Japanese, Hebrew, French and German. They range from the mundane ("Tom Walker wuz here") to the profane (pictures of John in an act that shall remain unnamed) and from the average fan ("The Beatles rule—my fave band, from Jackie") to the die-hards ("Yesterday is so much better thanks to you, from Peter").

Be warned: Abbey Road Studios has no visitors' facilities. While the staff smile rather symphathetically at the earnest and eager fans who try to enter, they politely suggest a visit to the rather disappointing and tiny Abbey Road Cafe (attached to the St. John's Wood tube on Finchley Road, ☎ 020 7586 5404).

LEXY BLOOM
Writer and editor

5.14 Lord's Cricket Ground

St. John's Wood NW8, 020 7289 1611
St. John's Wood

Note the general architecture, especially the new stand built by Michael Hopkins (1985–1987). Delicious Indian flavour reminiscent of New Delhi. I played there many times as a schoolboy and from Oxford and having been brought up in Calcutta, always felt a pang of recognition.

Alas, the new media centre, looking as if it had just landed from outer space, is out of keeping (built by Future Systems, 1995–1998).

ALAN ROSS (1922–2001)
Author and editor

5.15 The Shaker Shop

72 Marylebone High Street W1, 020 7935 9461
Baker Street, Regent's Park

When the private views are getting me down, I go and look at The Shaker Shop on the Marylebone High Street: inside if open; the windows if not. Shaker chairs are a fabulous example of "form and function" in design—they were originally intended as "chairs for angels to sit in;" today, they are slightly more robust in construction (this fourteen stone rector couldn't sit on one otherwise) but still magic. Shaker design is a tonic. Sometimes, I even buy things there.

CHRISTOPHER FRAYLING
Rector, Royal College of Art

RECOMMENDED READING
June Sprigg, *Shaker Design*, Whitney Museum of American Art, 1986.

5.16 Ravi Shankar Restaurant

133 Drummond Street NW1, 020 7388 6458
Euston

When I lived in Notting Hill Gate, I used to like to go alone to the Baba Bhelpoori House where South Indian vegetarian food was served. Then the restaurant closed down and anyhow I moved away. Now I live in Camden Town and I have discovered that, in a little grid of streets my side of the Euston Road, there is an entire little village devoted to South Indian vegetarian restaurants. My favourite is the Ravi Shankar Restaurant, opposite the Islamic Book Centre. Many Moslems live or work in the area and there is a mosque one street away from the restaurant. I love the food, particularly the *bhelpoori*, a dish made apparently of spicy rice crispies and yoghurt, and it has the additional advantage of being extremely cheap. I also like the area, which is an oasis of calm marooned between the Euston Road and Camden.

LUCRETIA STEWART
Writer and journalist

A Film Buff's Stroll

The Holmes and the Hannay Walks

Start at the BBC Broadcasting House, which is located at Portland Place W1, ☏ 020 8743 8000

⊖ Regent's Park, Oxford Circus

For thirty years I worked at Broadcasting House near Oxford Circus, and lived first on the west side of Hampstead Heath, then on the east side, and would often walk the three miles home via Camden Town. The first journey is the one Sherlock Holmes and Dr Watson took from Oxford Street to Hampstead in *The Adventures of Charles Augustus Milverton* to burgle the home of the "king of all blackmailers," who lived at a Gothic mansion on the corner of East Heath Road and Well Road. They subsequently fled from the house, zig-zagging across the Heath to emerge presumably on the Highgate Road and catch a cab back to Baker Street.

The second journey is the one walked by the intrepid Richard Hannay in John Buchan's classic conspiracy thriller *The Three Hostages*, just after World War I, following the first clue that leads him from Oxford Circus via Camden Town to Gospel Oak at the Heath's southeast corner. His walk takes him past the apartment block at 122 Portland Place from which Hannay would later escape, disguised as a milkman in Hitchcock's *The 39 Steps*.

The most sublime Hitchcock image from the 1930s is of the unattended horse-drawn milk-float in Park Crescent. You can get to Camden Town by the Nash Terraces of Regent's Park's Outer Circle or Albany Street, from the top of which, at the White House, the Soviet spy Gordon Lonsdale ran his espionage ring in the 1960s. Camden Town is where the nine-year-old Charles Dickens lived in Bayham Street, as well as being the home of the Cratchit family in *A Christmas Carol* and the inner-city area transformed by the coming of the railways in *Dombey and Son*. At Parkway, Camden Town is Palmer's Pet Store above which the Communist leader Bennett lived in Graham Greene's *It's a Battlefield*.

Going North by the Holmes or the Hannay route takes you through George Orwell territory—in the mid-30s he lived in Warwick Mansions, Pond Street, 77 Parliament Hill, and 50 Lawford Road, Kentish Town, and worked at a bookshop called Booklover's Corner (immortalised in *Keep the Aspidistra Flying*) in South End Green, as recorded by a plaque on the corner. At Gospel Oak you'll reach Gordon House Road, along which a psychopathic hitman drives on his way to a killing on the opening page of Ruth Rendell's *The Lake of Darkness*. Cross over to the Heath and climb to the top of Parliament Hill where D. H. Lawrence and Frieda watched zeppelins bombing London in World War I, as described in *Kangaroo*.

PHILIP FRENCH
Film critic and broadcaster

BLOOMSBURY
& KING'S CROSS

6
Crowndale Road
Mornington Crescent
Oakley Square
Pancras Road
Camley Street
York Way
King's Cross Station
Hampstead Road
Polygon Rd.
Barnby St.
Brill Place
Midland Road
Ossulston Street
St. Pancras Station
King's Cross St. Pancras
Chalton St.
Euston Station
Cardington Street
Eversholt Street
Euston
Hastings Street
Judd Street
Cartwright Gardens
Euston Road
Endsleigh Gdns.
Burton St.
Drummond Street
Euston Square
Gordon Street
Hunter St.
Tavistock Square
Tavistock Pl.
Gower Street
Gordon Square
Woburn Place
Herbrand Street
Handel Street
Warren Street
Bedford Way
Woburn Square
Bernard
Russell Square
Tottenham Court Road
Grafton Way
Fitzroy Square
Fitzroy Street
Whitfield Street
Southampton
Maple Street
Howland Street
Chenies Street
Montague Place
Great Titchfield Street
Cleveland Street
Tottenham Street
Goodge Street
Great Portland Street
Foley Street
Riding House Street
Charlotte Street
Bedford Square
Great Russell St.
Little Russell Street
Muse Street
Percy Street
Mortimer Street
Newman Street
Rathbone Place
Berners Street
Hanway Gate
New Oxford Street
Bloomsbury Way
Regent Street
Oxford Circus
Oxford Street
Soho Square
St. Giles High St.
High Holborn
Charing Cross Rd
Great Marlborough Street
1
5
6
7
8
9
10
11
12
13
14
17

BLOOMSBURY & KING'S CROSS

1 Gandhi Memorial
2 The Foundling Museum
3 Coram's Fields
4 St. George's Gardens
5 St. Pancras Station and the former Midland Grand Hotel
6 St. Pancras Old Church
7 The British Library
8 The Birdcage Restaurant
9 The Goldbeater's Building
10 Back to Basics
11 Contemporary Applied Arts
12 Charlotte Street Hotel
13 The British Museum
14 St. George's
15 Sir John Soane's Museum
16 The Royal College of Surgeons
17 Ladbrokes Casino (see p. 75)

BLOOMSBURY & KING'S CROSS

6.1 Gandhi Memorial

1968, Fredda Brilliant

Tavistock Square WC1

Euston, Russell Square

When I'm stressed out in Bloomsbury—it can happen—a good place to realign the energies is with this bronze Mahatma. He's just sitting there on top of the stone table/cave/plinth that always seems to have fresh flower offerings. The traffic and all that noise becomes the background and the memorial gives you back to yourself with gentleness and strength.

ANTONY GORMLEY
Sculptor

6.2 The Foundling Museum

Original building, 1741 by Theodore Jacobsen; current building, 1937–1938 by J.M. Sheppard.

40 Brunswick Square WC1, 020 7841 3600

Currently not open to the public; call for additional information.

 Russell Square

Thomas Coram, a rich sea captain, came back to London from a voyage and was shocked to see so many beggars and street urchins living rough in the midst of the city's bustle and prosperity—children who were the predecessors of Fagin's gang and *Les Misèrables*. The Foundling Hospital, near Coram Fields, which he founded in 1742, now houses the Coram Foundation and its fine collection of paintings—put together originally by none other than William Hogarth. He was a friend of Coram's and painted the magnificent portrait of him. But the orphanage is worth a visit above all to see the poignant tokens the mothers left with their babies: buttons scratched with their names, scraps of ribbon, clipped coins, and poems.

MARINA WARNER
Writer

Everything about this collection of 18th-century painting, sculpture, furniture and memorabilia is extraordinary from its origins to the fact that it is still together and still little known. It only exists because the retired sea captain, Thomas Coram, was so appalled by the state of London's neglected street children that he spent the rest of his life setting up The Foundling Hospital, and because he was so good at enthusing other people like Hogarth and Handel to help, that it became *the* fashionable cause. From 1750 Handel conducted annual performances of *The Messiah* in the Hospital Chapel. Roubiliac's terra cotta bust of him, and the keyboard of the organ he gave, form part of the collection, to which Hogarth, Ramsay, Reynolds, and Gainsborough all contributed. When women handed over their babies to the care of the hospital they often attached tokens to identify them, in case changed circumstances should ever allow them to reclaim their lost children. This did occasionally happen, but the display of unreclaimed pins, chains, ribbons, hearts, coins, and other items, speak poignantly of the more usual outcome.

The difficulty with recommending this collection is that at the moment you can only visit it by arranging it with the museum a long time in advance. If the desired funding is found it will then become impossible to visit after April 2001, during refurbishment, but thereafter (2003) the whole thing will be open properly. Meanwhile, I would suggest reading *Coram's Children, The London Foundling Hospital in the Eighteenth Century* by Ruth McClure, and taking a walk round the area of Coram's Fields.

RUTH PAVEY
Reviewer, journalist, and teacher

RECOMMENDED READING

Ruth McClure, *Coram's Children, The London Foundling Hospital in the Eighteenth Century*, Yale University Press, 1981.

6.3 Coram's Fields

93 Guilford Street WC1, ☎ 020 7837 6138
The park is a five-minute walk east of Russell Square.
⊖ Russell Square

Visiting London with young children can be difficult. The traffic, the appalling public transport, the hostile restaurant staff, can all add up to an extremely trying experience. Yet there are a few oases, even in central London. One of these is Coram's Fields: a lovely children's park five minutes' walk east of Russell Square. The entrance is on Guilford Street, where a sign on an iron gate states, with a gentle ironic twist, "No adults unaccompanied by children." The park was originally part of a foundling hospital, built in the early 18th century by the philanthropist Thomas Coram. You enter to find an unexpectedly large expanse of green, dotted with majestic plane trees and flanked on either side by rows of miniature Palladian columns. It's easy to imagine that you've entered the grounds of an 18th-century estate, save for the all-weather football pitch at the far end.

The park contains a variety of facilities for children: swings, monkey gyms, and a range of other energy-sapping constructions. In addition to this, the park keeps animals, mostly chicken and sheep, which roam around an enclosed area adding to the bucolic calm and amusing the children no end. For very young children there is the "under fives club," where parents can get a cup of tea or coffee and the kids can play with each other and an impressive variety of toys. The professional carers on site are charming and helpful, and there are clean changing facilities. Once you've explored the fields take a walk down Lamb's Conduit, straight out the gate at the south end of the park and across Guilford Street at the Zebra Crossing. There are some interesting shops and a number of very good cafes on this street, as well as one of the best preserved and run pubs in central London, appropriately known as The Lamb (94 Lamb's Conduit, 020 7405 0713).

RICHARD NOBLE
Political philosopher

6.4

St. George's Gardens

Opened in 1715; laid out as a public open space in 1885.
Handel Street WC1
Russell Square

From 1713 to about 1850 this was a burial ground attached to the church of St. George the Martyr, Queen's Square and also for St. George, Bloomsbury. It reopened as a public garden in 1882 designed by William Holmes. Until some years ago it was a pleasure to walk through it, from Sidmouth Street to Handel Street, under big plane trees, past graves and the terra cotta muse who stood alone in a flower bed. Then, in the era of Thatcherite economies, the gardens were neglected and the muse had her hand broken off. By late September 2001, however, all should be well, with the graves tidied up, the early 19th-century chapel of ease restored, a new planting of Indian Bean trees, winter box and herbaceous perennials, and the muse's hand, preserved by a local man, given back to her.

RUTH PAVEY
Reviewer, journalist and teacher

Old St. Pancras

Euston, King's Cross/St. Pancras

6.5

St. Pancras Station and the former Midland Grand Hotel

Train shed, 1863–1867 by W. H. Barlow and R. M. Ordish; hotel, from 1868–1872 by Sir George Gilbert Scott; used as offices after 1935.
Euston Road NW1

6.6

St. Pancras Old Church

Parts date back to 600 AD; church restored in 1847–1848 by A. D. Gough and R. L. Roumieu.

Pancras Road NW1

Echoes of the railway age can be discerned at any of London's stations (the grim bunker of Euston excepted), but for Gothic grandeur and industrial muscle, none compare to St. Pancras. The ornate redbrick façade of Sir Gilbert Scott's Midland Grand Hotel, topped with a cluster of fantastical spires and bustling chimneys, remains one of London's most popular landmarks, and its lofty spirit now jeers at the new British Library opposite (see p. 102).

Plans to restore the Midland Hotel are regularly announced but the building remains empty; a scandal, for its sweeping staircases and ironwork traceries are as remarkable as its exterior. You can, however, still enjoy a ticket hall modelled on a medieval cloister and marvel at the vast iron arch of William Barlow's station, which was completed in 1868, seven years before Scott's hotel. Below both lie the vaults where Burton-on-Trent beer was once stored but which now house occasional car boot sales.

The area behind St. Pancras Station and its less imposing neighbour, King's Cross, is rich in atmosphere and history, if in little else. It used to be called Battle Bridge, this being where the recalcitrant Queen Boudicca led the Iceni to their doom against Caesar's legions. Legend has her buried beneath Platform Seven of St. Pancras.

It's the age of Victoria which haunts Battlebridge Road, where the soot of the steam era has yet to be scrubbed from its tenements, courts, looming bridges and gasometers. All are stars of innumerable films, from *Ladykillers* to *High Hopes*, and most lie under threat of demolition as the 125 acres of railway land behind the stations await their much deferred fate. At least Norman Foster's 1989 plan to flatten the graceful curve of the Great Northern Hotel remains scuppered.

Wander up Pancras Road, past the car-washes and bakeries that occupy the vast arches beneath the track, and you'll find St. Pancras Old Church, allegedly one of London's most ancient holy sites, and named after a fourth-century martyr. The mediaeval church was restored beyond salvation by Victorian do-gooders, but its churchyard, its garden freshly planted, is a treasure. Forging the Midland line required levelling the old, tightly packed burial ground, and a scandal arose when early passengers espied bones and skulls poking from the trackside. The young Thomas Hardy helped relocate the remains and gravestones, many of which are swirled and stacked around the churchyard's London planes, and later wrote about it:

We late lamented, resting here,
Are mixed to human jam,
And each to each exclaims in fear,
'I know not which I am.'
—*Thomas Hardy*

Somewhere below, along with the uncharted dead, lies the buried Fleet River, whose passage from Hampstead to the Thames is now contained entirely in an iron pipe. Of the "spa and wells" of old St. Pancras, there is no sign.
NEIL SPENCER
Journalist and scriptwriter

Victorian London was based around railway stations. Euston (now a 1970s building), St. Pancras and King's Cross are all within a five-minute walk, servicing the north of England and Scotland. Head for St. Pancras and admire the station and its hotel, then walk north passing the New British Library, the Gas Works and warehouses. The dark and gloom symbolize beautifully Dickensian London—just wander, preferably with mist or rain—you really will catch what it is like.
LEX FENWICK
Managing Director-Europe, Bloomberg LP

6.7 The British Library

1999, Colin St. John Wilson & Partners
96 Euston Road NW1, 020 7412 7332
Euston, King's Cross/St. Pancras

The British are good at renovating or restoring old buildings, but less good at building new ones. The exception is the unashamedly modern British Library by Sir Colin St. John Wilson at St. Pancras. The outside is not to everyone's taste but stand in the piazza off Euston Road by the Paolozzi statue of Newton and look towards the Gothic extravaganza of St. Pancras Station. Inside the library, you'll find the finest public space created in the United Kingdom in the late 20th century, filled with works by living British artists: a Kitaj tapestry, a Woodrow scuplture and a Patrick Hughes picture. There are incomparable exhibition galleries with the Magna Carta, Beatles manuscripts and more. All free.
JOHN M. ASHWORTH
Chairman, British Library Board

RECOMMENDED READING
Colin St. John Wilson, *The Design and Construction of the British Library*, The British Library, 1998.

Seating yourself in Humanities II, seat number 3189 or 3183 (whichever is available), then staring into the space in front of you at about 45 degrees and upwards provides you with one of the clearest and most peaceful spaces in London. Use ear plugs if you feel there's too much noise from laptop keyboard activity behind you, or too much map rustling from the mezzanine above. Take out about twenty centimeters of books (through randomly selecting a keyword on the library computer index) which you must stack unread on the table in front of you. Then begin concentrating on the spectacular light changes within the space upwards and ahead of you. 4pm–7pm should be ideal.
ADAM CHODZKO
Artist

Epitaph for a Library

Yesterday I received proof that my cosy and beloved London refuge would be irrevocably confiscated from me. I entered the Reading Room of the Library, in the heart of the British Museum, and instead of the usual warm atmosphere I was greeted with a distressing spectacle: half of the vast shelves surrounding the room had been emptied and in place of the elegant rows of thousands of bound books, I saw discolored wood, some of it stained with what seemed to be cobwebs. I don't think I've felt such a sense of betrayal since, upon turning five years old, my mother took me to the La Salle School of Cochabamba and abandoned me in Brother Justinian's classroom.

I came to this place for the first time 32 years ago, newly arrived in London, to read books by Edmund Wilson, whose essay about the evolution of socialism—*To The Finland Station*—had touched me. Before I could notice the richness of its collection—about nine million volumes—I was dazzled by the beauty of the main Reading Room, covered by those shelves smelling of leather and paper and submerged in a blue light that discreetly descended upon her from the incredible dome built by Sidney Smirke in 1857, the largest in the world next to that of the Pantheon in Rome, which exceeds it only by two feet in diameter. Since I was accustomed to working in impersonal and uncomfortable libraries, like that of Paris—always so crowded that during the exams period you had to stand in line in the Place de la Bourse for an hour before it opened to be admitted—I couldn't believe that this one, besides being so beautiful, was so comfortable, so quiet and hospitable, with its fluffy seats and long tables where you could spread out your notebooks, index cards, and high stacks of books without cramping your neighbors. It was here old Marx had spent a good part of his life, according to Wilson, and where in the sixties his desk was still preserved to the right of the entrance, but which in the mid-eighties disappeared with all the desks in that row in order to make room for computers.

Without exaggeration, I can say that I have spent four or five afternoons a week in the Reading Room of the British Library during all of my stays in London over three decades, and that here I have been extremely happy, more so than in any other place in the world. Here, lulled by the quiet hum of the carts that hand out their orders to each reader, and calmed by the intimate security that no phone nor bell would ring, and no visitor would drop by, I would prepare my literature classes when I taught at Queen Mary College and at King's College; here I've written letters, articles, essays, plays, and a half-dozen novels. And here I've read hundreds of books thanks to which I've learned almost everything I know. But mostly in this place I've fantasized and dreamt about the great thinkers, of the formidable illusionists, of the masters of fiction.

I became used to working in the library since my University days, and in every place I have lived, I have been able to continue doing so, such that my memories of the countries and cities are in good measure shaped by the images and anecdotes that I retain of their libraries. The old big house of San Marcos had a dense and colonial air and the books exhaled a light dust that made one sneeze. In the National Library, on Abancay Avenue, the schoolchildren made an infernal noise, as did the monitors, who would shush them (or emulate them, rather) with shrill whistles. In the National Club, where I worked, I read an entire erotic collection *Les Maitres de l'Amour*, directed, introduced, and translated by Guillaume Apollinaire. In the freezing National Library of Madrid, toward the end of the fifties, you had to wear a coat so as not to get sick, but I went there every afternoon to read the novels of chivalry. The library in Paris was so uncomfortable it surpassed all the others: if you accidentally moved your arm away from your body, you would elbow your neighbor in the ribs. There, one afternoon, I raised my eyes from a crazy book, about crazy people, *Les Enfants du Limon* by Raymond Queneau, and I came face to face with Simone de Beauvoir, who was sitting right in front of me, writing furiously.

The greatest surprise I had with regard to libraries was with an erudite Chilean in charge of the acquisition of Spanish American books in the Library of Congress in Washington. In 1965 I asked him what the criteria was for acquiring books and he responded: "Very easy. We buy all the books that are published." This was also the millionaire policy of the formidable library at Harvard, where one had to go alone to search for a book following a complicated itinerary traced by the computer, which acted as a receptionist. In the semester I spent there I never managed to orient myself in that labyrinth, I never could read what I wanted, I just wandered through the belly of the bibliographic whale, but I can't complain because I made some wonderful finds, such as the memoirs of Herzen—a Russian liberal—and *The Octopus* by Frank Norris.

One snowy afternoon in the library at Princeton, while taking advantage of the carelessness of my neighbor, I spied a book he was reading and found a quote about the cult of Dionysus in Ancient Greece, which lead me to completely change the novel I was writing and attempt an Andean, modern recreation of that classic myth about irrational forces and divine intoxication. In the New York Public Library, the most efficient of all—you don't need a membership, the books you need are brought to you in minutes—and with the hardest seats, it was impossible to work for more than a few hours straight unless you brought a small pillow to protect your tailbone.

I have nice memories of all these libraries and several others, but none of them, alone or separately, was able to help, stimulate and serve me as well as the Reading Room. Of the innumerable episodes with which I could illustrate this statement, I chose this one: to have found in its archives the most obscure little magazine that the Dominican priests of the Amazonian mission published there, in those remote lands, half a century ago, and that are one of the scarce testimonies about the Machiguengas, their myths, their legends, their customs, their language. I was desperately asking my friends from Lima that they find and photocopy them—I needed the material for a novel—and it turns out the complete collection was there, in the British Library, at my disposal.

When in 1978 the Labour Party announced that, due to a lack of space, a new library would be built and the Reading Room would be returned to the British Museum, a cold shiver ran through my spine. But I figured that, given the poor state of the British economy then, the costly project would take probably more than the years I had left in life to materialize. However, in the 1980s things started to get better in the United Kingdom and the new building, constructed in a neighborhood known above all for its ruffians and prostitutes, St. Pancras, began to grow and show its horrendous brick face and prison-like grates. The historian Hugh Thomas formed a committee to try to convince the authorities that, although the British Library was moving to the new space, they should preserve the Reading Room of the British Museum. I was one of its members and I wrote letters and signed manifestos that were completely pointless, because the British Museum was determined to recapture what *de jure* belonged to it, and its influence and arguments prevailed over our own.

Now, all is lost. The books have already been taken to St. Pancras and although in theory this Reading Room will remain open until mid-October and a month later the Humanities Room will open in its place, this one has already begun to die, slowly, since they ripped out the soul which gave it life, the books, and they left a large empty shell. Those few sentimentalists of us left will continue coming here until the last day, just as one accompanies a loved one in their last days of agony, in order to be with them until the final death rattle. But nothing will be the same these months, neither the hushed hustle and bustle of days gone by, nor that comfortable sensation with which one could read, research, take notes and write, possessed by a curious state of mind, that of having escaped the wheel of time, of having consented to that concave space of blue light and to that timelessness of the life of books, and that of ideas and of the admirable fantasies incarnated in them.

Of course, in the nearly twenty years it's taken to be built, the St. Pancras Library has turned out too small and will be unable to house all of its collections, which will be dispersed in different storage spaces strewn throughout London. And the defects and deficiencies that seem to afflict it have caused the *Times Literary Supplement* to describe it as "The British Library or The Great Disaster." I, of course, have not visited it and when I pass by I look at the brave prostitutes on the sidewalks, and not at its rocky and bloody walls, reminiscent of banks, barracks or electrical plants, not of intellectual endeavors. I, of course, will not step foot inside until I have no choice, and will continue proclaiming until my death that, by replacing that beloved place with this horror, a shameful crime has been committed—and one that is quite explicable. After all, aren't these the same people who sent poor Oscar Wilde to jail and who banned Joyce's *Ulysses* and Lawrence's *Lady Chatterley's Lover*?

MARIO VARGAS LLOSA
Writer
Written in London, June, 1997; translated by Paula Bloom

6.8 **The Birdcage Restaurant**
110 Whitfield Street WC1, ☎ 020 7383 3346
⊖ Warren Street

For a long comfortable evening, with lots of surprises, do go to this small exotic restaurant which is the absolute antithesis of "cool" London. Decorated with paintings, peacock feathers, antiques and bird cages, it holds very few tables but each one seems to be decorated individually. There are strange toys to play with and the menus come within battered old novels. The food is imaginative and there are delicious breads and sorbets before and between courses. We stayed for ages.

MARGARET RICHARDSON
Curator

The Historic Squares of London

London Historic Parks and Gardens Trust, Duck Island Cottage, St. James's Park
For recorded information in weeks leading up to Open Squares Day, 020 7839 3969

For the last three years, on the second Sunday in June, about sixty private squares in London have opened to the public, ranging from the squares of Bloomsbury to the Grosvenor Estate (e.g., Belgrave Square) and the private square gardens of the Ladbroke Estate. Out of central London, squares such as Merrick Square, in Southwark (and part of the corporation of Trinity House) and Albion Square (part of the Saumarez Estate in Hackney), open their gates to the public, showing beautiful, small, landscaped sites.

IMOGEN MAGNUS
Writer and researcher

6.9 The Goldbeater's Building

1919, Ernest H. Abbott
54–60 Whitfield Street W1
Warren Street, Goodge Street

The area called Fitzrovia, to the north of Oxford Street and west of Tottenham Court Road, is famous for its early 20th-century artists and writers—Augustus John, Walter Sickert, Wyndham Lewis, George Orwell and many others. Little note is made of the area's interesting industries, but one of these was the production of gold leaf.

George Manning Whiley was a goldbeater and since 1896 had worked in Whitfield Street. He grew wealthy and commissioned an interesting building, now called the Goldbeater's Building, from an architect by the name of Ernest H. Abbott, about whom almost nothing is known. The façade has decorative capitals that incorporate tools of the goldbeaters' trade. The building was completed in 1919 and has passed through many hands since Whiley's day. Local residents have fought against its demolition and have asked that it be returned to "light industrial" use. It is now under a conservation order but occupied by office desks and fax machines.

MICHELE FIELD
Writer and journalist

6.10 **Back to Basics**
21A Foley Street W1, 020 7436 2181
Weekdays only
Goodge Street

This is an unpretentious fish restaurant, located in a lively pocket of bars and restaurants which are less well-known than those on Charlotte Street. In the summer, there are tables outside which quickly fill with BBC lunchers. Gypsy bands come serenading and a colony of seagulls living inexplicably in the area create the illusion of a harbour nearby. Without being deliberately retro, the interior has the chirpy innocence of the 1970s, and the food is always deliciously fresh. There are no great tourist sites in Fitzrovia, but it's a good place to head after exploring Bloomsbury or to get away from shopping crowds.

OPHELIA FIELD
Writer and journalist

Shops as Galleries

3.3 **Egg, Contemporary Craft and Clothing**
36 Kinnerton Street SW1, 020 7235 9315

11.13 **Livingstone Studio**
36 New End Square, NW3, 020 7431 6311

6.11 **Contemporary Applied Arts**
2 Percy Street W1, 020 7436 2344

6.12 **Charlotte Street Hotel**
15–17 Charlotte Street W1, 020 7907 4000)

There are some shops which are almost art galleries, and if you come only to look, you look with a different "eye" than when you look at priceless (or unpriced) pieces in a museum. Egg in South Kensington and Livingstone Studio in Hampstead are two such shops but my favorite is Contemporary Applied Arts in Fitzrovia. This "shop" has seven seasons each year, each season six or seven weeks long. Everything on the two floors changes with each season, much as it would in a commercial art gallery. There is background to read for each object, as in a museum—so you buy a provenance, no matter how practical the teapot or how "everyday" the earrings. And you can buy postcards showing what you might have acquired if money or space were no object.

Contemporary Applied Arts is at the bottom end of Charlotte Street on the corner with Percy. This is media-central, with CNN and Pearson's and dozens of film and television companies within sight of one another. After a visit to Contemporary Applied Arts, enjoy a drink at the Charlotte Street Hotel, a building which once housed London's biggest supplier of dentists' chairs and drills—and opened in 2000 as a gentlemanly hub (as opposed to gentleman's club) for the arts and media.

MICHELE FIELD
Writer and journalist

6.13 The British Museum

1823–1852, Sir Robert Smirke and others

Great Russell Street WC1, 020 7636 1555

Russell Square, Holborn, Tottenham Court Road

"A foggy day in London town. . .
I viewed the morning with alarm,
The British Museum had lost its charm. . ."
—*Ira Gershwin*

These lyrics from "A Foggy Day" have to be among the most ironic in popular music: nobody could ever find the severely imposing British Museum charming under any circumstances. In the peace following the Napoleonic period Britain commissioned Smirke to design the massive neo-classical pile to house the collections of art and antiquities bequeathed to the nation in the late 18th and early 19th centuries. Over the years numerous other architects, most recently Norman Foster, have made improvements and alterations. Fragments of the Temple of Artemis at Ephesus, one of the canonical Seven Wonders of the World, are displayed in Room 3. At night the orange sodium floodlights render the refined Ionic façade wildly Asiatic and pagan.

PETER J. HOLLIDAY
Historian

Though obviously a standard attraction for most tourists, the British Museum is my favorite because of its enormous collections covering over 2.5 miles of galleries! The Greek, Roman, Egyptian and Near-Eastern collections are among the finest in the world—appropriate for the oldest public museum in the world. Among its other superb collections are the great "treasures" of the migration period and illuminated manuscripts, the Oriental Art collection and the new Mexican/Pre-Columbian art gallery. It would take days to discover all of its treasures, not to mention visiting its always excellent temporary and visiting exhibitions.

SUSAN SILBERBERG-PIERCE
Art historian and photographer

The wealth of the collection is always startling and rejuvenating. Also, they have good ice cream in front.
SUSAN KLEINBERG
Artist

The Great Court

A must is Norman Foster's new Great Court hidden away inside the British Museum and just open. The old Reading Room is restored to its former glory in the centre. All is transformed, sparkling under the ingenious new doughnut glazed roof: intricate shadows criss-cross the cream stone façades of the court when the sun is out.

The museum has become much more accessible: a joy, especially when remembering previous labyrinthine routes when working on British Museum installations.
LADY STIRLING (AKA MARY SHAND)
Designer

Museum Trails

Visiting museums with children, an activity that so often takes on the character of a forced march, is most enjoyable in London, where all of the major galleries—and many of the small ones—provide a particularly British item called "trails." For Americans unfamiliar with the term, these are simple guides through the museums especially geared to children. Available at the front desk, they are usually free (and never more than a few pence) and range from handsomely-produced full-colour brochures (the Royal Academy's Hiroshige trail of several years ago comes to mind) or a few xeroxed pages (the Wallace Collection). At best, they provide the excitement of a treasure hunt; at the very least, they point parents in the direction of pieces in the collection most likely to appeal to children.

Over the years, our family has devised our own trails of artworks in three favorite museums: the British Museum, The National Gallery and the National Portrait Gallery.

6.13 **The British Museum**

Great Russell Street WC1, 020 7636 1555 (see p. 111)

The crowds are overwhelming, but it's worth soldiering through to view The Mildenhall Treasure. Beforehand, be sure to read Roald Dahl's riveting account of the discovery of this Roman silver—the greatest treasure ever found in the British Isles—by a farmer plowing his field in Suffolk in 1942, and of the treachery that ensued. In addition, don't miss the greatest surviving set of mediaeval chessmen. Most enthralling of all, however, is The Lindow Man: the body of a murdered prehistoric man discovered under a peat bog and now enhanced by a hologram which lends an unearthly glimmer. His body dates back to the Iron Age—mid-first century AD—and he was found in 1985 in Lindow Moss, Cheshire, England. He's affectionately called "Pete Marsh" and we've found it nearly impossible to tear ourselves away from him in less than twenty minutes.

1.2 **The National Gallery**

Trafalgar Square WC2, 020 7747 2885 (see p. 12)

While not particularly bloodthirsty in real life, our children nonetheless have never tired of visiting: *Perseus turning Phineas and his Followers to Stone* by Luca Giordano (about 1680); *Belshazzar's Feast* by Rembrandt (about 1635) with its terrifying judgement in Hebrew: "You have been weighed in the balances and have been found wanting;" and the endlessly alluring *Samson and Delilah* by Peter Paul Rubens (about 1609).

If parents can recount the stories behind the paintings, following a Biblical trail is another way to wend your way through the galleries. Here are some dramatic moments:

The Agony in the Garden by Andrea Mantegna (about 1460); *The Stigmatisation of Saint Francis*, part of *The Life of Saint Francis*, by Sassetta (1437–1444); *Christ Driving the Traders from the Temple* by El Greco (about 1600); *Saint Jerome in a Rocky Landscape* attributed to Joachim

Patinir (about 1515–1524); *Joseph with Jacob in Egypt* by Jacopo Pontormo (about 1518); *The Raising of Lazarus* by Sebastiano del Piombo (about 1517–1519); *Christ Washing the Feet of his Disciples* by Jacopo Tintoretto (about 1556); *The Supper at Emmaus* by Caravaggio (1601), with the teetering fruit basket about to fall onto the floor of the National Gallery; *Christ Before the High Priest* by Gerrit van Honthorst (about 1617); and *The Finding of Moses* by Nicolas Poussin (1651).

A warning note: We've always found *A Grotesque Old Woman*, attributed to Quinten Massys (about 1525–1530), much too creepy, especially for the six and unders. Avoid it.

1.5

National Portrait Gallery

2 St. Martin's Place WC2, ☎ 020 7306 0055 (see p. 15)

One way to enjoy this lovely, moving collection is to purchase select postcards in the gift shop beforehand, then hand them to the children and ask them to find the corresponding paintings. (Ask the children not to turn over the postcard and read the subject's name before finding it.) Younger children will be charmed to discover Beatrix Potter, J. R. R. Tolkien and A. A. Milne and Christopher Robin Milne with Winnie the Pooh. Another great conversation piece is the portrait of Edward VI, the little prince who ascended to the throne at age nine and was immortalized in Mark Twain's *The Prince and the Pauper*. No child will fail to be moved by the story of the prince who changed places with a poor boy just for a trial, but whose life might have changed permanently, were it not for the deep faith of the one, and the sincere honesty of the other.

Older children will be intrigued by the portraits of Charles Dickens, the Brontes, Charles Darwin, Lord Byron, Elton John, Paul McCartney and a host of others.

ANGELA HEDERMAN
Editor and publisher

RECOMMENDED READING
Roald Dahl, 'The Mildenhall Treasure' in *The Wonderful Story of Henry Sugar and Six More*, Puffin Books, 1988.

6.14 St. George's

1718–1720, Nicholas Hawksmoor
Bloomsbury Way WC1, 020 7405 3044
Holborn, Tottenham Court Road

The neighbouring buildings are so close to the site that one can easily miss Hawksmoor's magnificent Portland stone Corinthian portico and steeple on this busy street. Largely unrestored, soot smoked and with weeds growing from its cornices, it has some of the grandeur of Rome, even of the portico of the Pantheon. It is of course smaller, as this is London, and 18th-century High Baroque. The design of the stepped steeple is based on Pliny's description of the Mausoleum of Halicarnassus (353 BC). It is topped by more Corinthian columns and a statue of George I as St. George, but in Roman dress, as one can see in Hogarth's engraving "Gin Lane."

Inside, the central space is nearly square, balanced, symmetrical, grand but plain, as was thought to befit the reformed English Church. There are carved brown oak fittings, moulded plasterwork, an altarpiece niche with cherubs and clouds in marquetry. (Imagine drawing, let alone making, this.) Otherwise stone—white and gold. It had been estimated to cost £9,790 but the final bill was £31,000. Well worth it.

DAVID MLINARIC
Interior designer and decorator

A Gothic church plan made with classical bits is swallowed by a classical temple. Note the difference between ceremonial and everyday entrance. Please, no hugging the over-scaled keystones in the base around the back.

ROBERT LIVESEY
Architect

6.15 Sir John Soane's Museum

1792–1824, Sir John Soane

13 Lincoln's Inn Fields WC2, 020 7405 2107

Holborn

One of the most idiosyncratic and memorable museums in the world, the perfectly preserved town house of the great Regency architect Sir John Soane (1753–1837) will always remain a revelation to those who are lucky enough to visit it for the first time. During a lifetime of collecting, Soane accumulated an amazing quantity of art works, historic fragments, plaster casts, drawings and models (many of the latter related to his own exceptional designs) and ingeniously placed them within a series of internal spaces covering the area of three standard Georgian terrace houses.

Using top-lighting, often with coloured glass, and a myriad of mirrors, he produced a setting of magical intensity where one is confronted within minutes by the alabaster sarcophagus of the Pharoah Seti I, Hogarth's pictorial drama of *A Rake's Progress*, Roman cinerary urns, medieval masonry from the Palace of Westminster, a cork model of an Etruscan tomb, and plaster casts of the *Apollo Belvedere* and *Medici Venus*. The Monk's Parlour, with its Gothic gloom, and the Picture Room, with layers of hinged walls housing a host of pictures and drawings (including melancholy Piranesi views of Paestum), constitute a mere sample of what awaits you.

JOHN WILTON-ELY
Art historian

RECOMMENDED READING

Gillian Darley, *John Soane: An Accidental Romantic*, Yale University Press, 1999.

Helen Dorey, '12–14 Lincoln's Inn Fields' in exhibition catalogue, *John Soane, Architect: Master of Space and Light*, Margaret Richardson and Mary Anne Stevens, eds., Royal Academy of Arts, London, distributed by Yale University Press, 1999.

Helen Dorey and Peter Thornton, *A Miscellany of Objects from Sir John Soane's Museum*, Laurence King, 1992.

John Wilton-Ely, *Piranesi at the Soane Museum*, Azimuth Editions, 2001.

ISLINGTON & CLERKENWELL

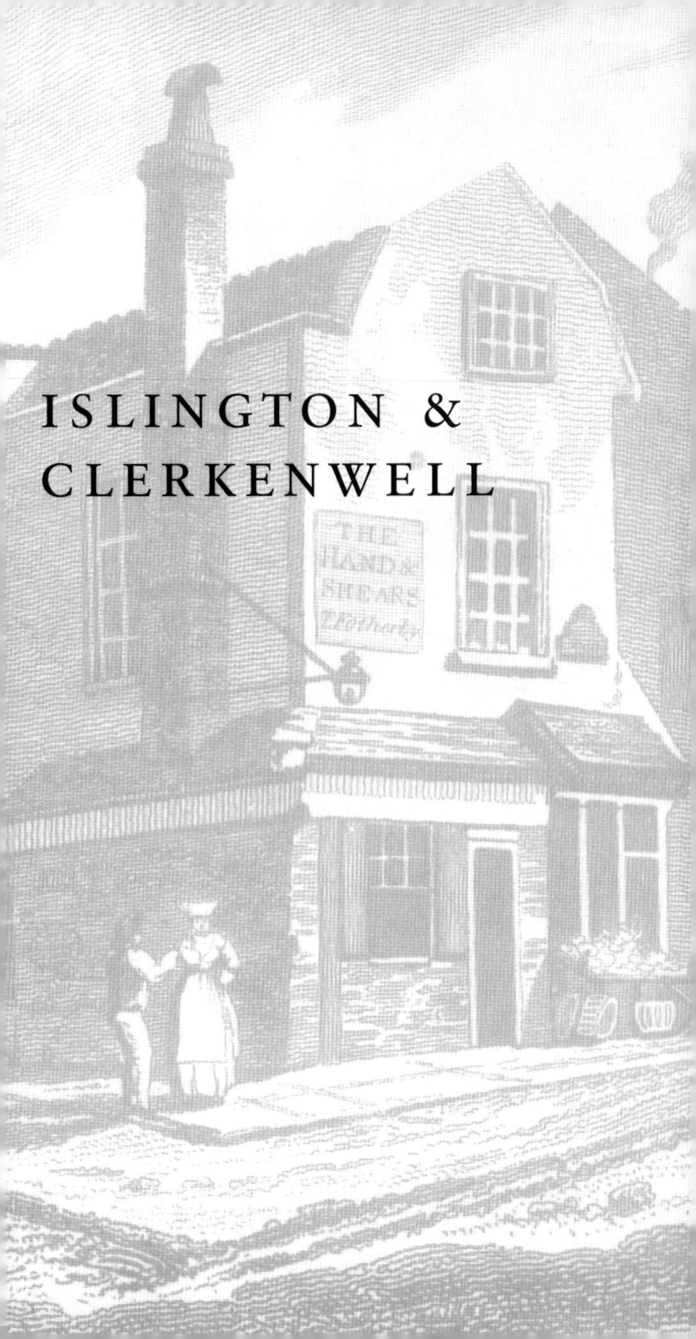

7
Barnard Park
Caledonian Road
Barnsbury Road
Cloudesley
Liverpool Road
Theburton St.
Upper Street
Essex Road
Packington Street
Chantry Street
St. Peter's Street
Charlton Place
Colebrooke Row
Tolpuddle Street
Chapel Market
Baron Street
Camden Passage
Gerrard Rd.
Noel Rd.
Duncan Terrace
Vincent Terrace
Angel
Elia St.
Graham St.
Pentonville Road
City Road
Goswell Road
Penton Rise
Amwell St.
Arlington Way
Percy Circus
Gt. Percy St.
Swinton Street
Acton Street
Wharton Street
Moreland St.
King's Cross
Rosebery Avenue
Spencer St.
Northampton Square
Gwynne Place
Wilmington Square
Myddelton Street
St. John Street
Skinner Street
Percival Street
Lever
Pine Street
Exmouth Market
Northampton Road
Calthorpe Street
Guilford St.
Rosebery Ave.
Farringdon Lane
Clerkenwell Green
Clerkenwell Road
Farringdon Road
Britton Street
Farringdon
Theobald's Road
Gray's Inn Gardens
Leather Lane
Hatton Garden
Barbican
Charterhouse Street
Long Lane
Aldersgate S
West Smithfield
Chancery Lane
High Holborn
Holborn
Shoe Lane
Holborn Viaduct
Smithfield
Lincoln's Inn Fields
Newgate St.
King Edward
St. Paul
1
2
3
4
5
6
7
8
9
10
11
12
13
14
15
16
17
18
19
20
21
22
23
24

ISLINGTON & CLERKENWELL

1 Postman's Park
2 St. Bartholomew's Hospital
3 St. Bartholomew-the-Great Church
4 Smithfield Market
5 St. John
6 Marx Memorial Library
7 Moro
8 Finsbury Health Centre
9 Spa Green Estate
10 Town Hall
11 Sadler's Wells Theatre
12 Family Records Centre
13 London Metropolitan Archives
14 Church of the Holy Redeemer
15 Quality Chop House
16 Gazzano's
17 Wilmington Square
18 Gwynne Place
19 Chapel Market
20 Colebrooke Cottage
21 55 Colebrooke Row
22 The Old Queen's Head
23 Camden Passage Antiques Market
24 Steve Hatt's Fishmongers

ISLINGTON & CLERKENWELL

Postman's Park

1900

King Edward Street EC1

St. Paul's

A minute away from St. Paul's Cathedral you can visit this tiny park during daylight hours. St. Botolph's Church next door is also worth a look.

I live nearby and discovered the park one day when I was walking my dog. The park is surrounded on all sides by buildings which makes it feel like a special, enclosed little patch of green in the city. It's surprisingly quiet most of the day. It has a few gravestones of marginal interest in that they're crammed up together in various parts of the park. It used to have a wonderful Michael Ayrton sculpture of a minotaur but a couple of years ago it was removed (having stood there since the 1970s) because it was deemed sacreligious or pagan by the church who presumably owns the land. It did have inordinately large genitals, I won't deny. I believe you can still find the sculpture elsewhere in the Barbican area.

However, the most arresting aspect of Postman's Park is the Watts Memorial. G. F. Watts was a painter of considerable repute in the late 19th century; he was also a philanthropist. He observed that most urban memorials honour the famous or the celebrated and campaigned for every major city in England to have a memorial to ordinary people. Neither government nor town planners, it seems, were interested in the idea so Watts paid for this memorial in London himself. There are no others to my knowledge.

It consists of a number of rather beautiful William Morris style plaques beneath a wooden canopy. Each one commemorates a "heroic act of self-sacrifice: children who drowned saving the lives of other children, firemen, policemen, even a music hall artiste who burnt saving a fellow 'turn.'"

The tablets are strangely poignant in their verbal formality and I find these words and the gesture of the memorial itself both moving and sentimental in equal measures. That the memorial abuts a modern block of flats adds, for me, to its curiosity value. There is nothing else quite like it in London.

When I was writing my play, *Closer*, I decided to send one of my characters to Postman's Park—indeed she took her name from one of the dead on Watts's memorial (Alice Ayres). I also set the last scene of the play in the park. After the production opened I received a letter from a member of the audience who had been inspired by the play to visit the park and the Watts Memorial. I was delighted. I hope it might delight you too.

PATRICK MARBER
Playwright

Watts Memorial

1900

In 1900, painter and sculptor George Frederick Watts paid for a national memorial to "heroes of everyday life". People are commemorated in beautifully painted, sentimental tiles, i.e. "Soloman Galaman: Aged 11, died of injuries September 6, 1901 after saving his little brother from being run over in Commercial Street: 'Mother, I saved him but I could not save myself.'" It's an intriguing, tranquil hideaway park near the City—in the churchyard of St. Botolph's Aldersgate, and with a lovely fountain. Next to the Museum of London, too.

ERICA WAGNER
Editor

7.2 St. Bartholomew's Hospital

West Smithfield EC1, ☎ 020 7377 7000, ext. 8152
⊖ St. Paul's, Barbican

Christ at the Pool of Bethesda and **The Good Samaritan**
1736–1737, William Hogarth

Staircase Hall in North Wing
The paintings can be viewed from St. Bartholomew's Hospital Museum, or special tours can be arranged for a fee.

Although Hogarth is a very well-known artist and some of his most famous and characteristic "Modern Moral Subjects" can be seen in London at Tate Britain and Sir John Soane's Museum, these large and ambitious oil paintings show a much less well-known aspect of his work. They decorate the staircase walls of the architect James Gibbs's northern block at St. Bartholomew's Hospital, which was rebuilt in the mid-1730s. Hogarth appropriately depicts biblical subjects of healing: *Christ at the Pool of Bethesda* and *The Good Samaritan*.

Hogarth was born next door to the hospital and his mother and sister were pensioners there; these pictures were painted by the artist free-of-charge when it looked likely that the commission might be given to one of the many foreign decorative painters working in England in the first half of the 18th century. Somewhat optimistically as it transpired, Hogarth thought their public display would lead to a rash of commissions of this sort for churches and other public buildings.

BRIAN ALLEN
Art historian

RECOMMENDED READING
Ronald Paulson, *Hogarth: His Life, Art and Times*, 2 vols., Yale University Press, 1971, o.p.

7.3 St. Bartholomew-the-Great Church

14th century
West Smithfield EC1, 020 7606 5171
Barbican

Smithfield Market on a Sunday afternoon feels like Londonis having a hangover; the bars and restaurants are quiet, the meat market is empty, and the hospital (St. Bartholomew's, the oldest in London, founded in 1123) the same. There is a church in the northwestern corner—St. Barts, featured in Hugh Grant's wedding to Duckface in *Four Weddings and a Funeral*, where you can stroll into an exquisite service (9am, 11am, 6:30pm, Sundays). They are very welcoming to strangers, the choir is excellent, and the church a beautifully preserved example of a City parish church—one of the few to survive the Great Fire.

IAN KELLY
Actor and writer

7.4 Smithfield Market

Charterhouse Street EC1
Market open Mondays through Fridays, 5am–9am; building accessible at all hours.
Farringdon, Barbican

This is a splendid and spectacular piece of architecture which has two distinct lives. In the daytime it is a bustling meat market with huge trucks rumbling in and out. At night it becomes one of London's most happening districts with a new and fashionable restaurant, Smith's of Smithfield (67–77 Charterhouse Street, 020 7236 6666) and one of the city's most highly acclaimed clubs, Fabric (77A Charterhouse Street, 020 7490 0444)—both right opposite the market. Fabulous views of the market and St. Paul's Cathedral from the top floor of Smith's.

LESLEY DOWNER
Writer

7.5 St. John

26 St. John Street EC1, 020 7251 0848
Farringdon

Run by Fergus Henderson, the space is an old smoke house adjacent to Smithfield Market and the food is very British (the sign a pig "nose to tail eating"). Excellent.

LADY STIRLING (AKA MARY SHAND)
Designer

7.6 Marx Memorial Library

1737

37a Clerkenwell Green EC1, 020 7253 1485

Farringdon

London is home to a good many libraries, but few have the radical lineage and charm of the Marx Memorial Library. Centred on the partly pedestrianised Clerkenwell Green, the library is located in what is referred to locally as Marx House, a Grade II listed 18th-century building that serves as a vessel for a microcosmic social history of London, housing in turn a charity school, various small workshops and storefronts, before becoming a public house and coffee rooms in the last quarter of the 19th century. These were in effect workmen's clubs where one could read the seditious and blasphemous literature long produced and distributed in and around the Green.

A home to radical reform clubs supported by John Stuart Mill and frequented by Eleanor Marx, the Twentieth Century Press took over lease of the building with the financial support of William Morris in 1892. The TCP produced many of the earliest English editions of the works of Marx and Engels and during his London exile, Lenin edited *Iskra*, the newspaper of Russian Social Democracy, from an office lent to him by the press. The library has preserved this office as the Lenin Room. Other than some original well-worn Lenin-lino, the library boasts a large fresco, painted by Jack Hastings in 1935 shortly after the library was founded, that depicts a heroic worker of the future overturning the economic chaos of the present. A charity supported by independent subscriptions, the Marx Memorial Library lends books which contain ideas that still deserve a wider circulation.

JOHN SLYCE
Writer and critic

7.7

Moro

34–36 Exmouth Market EC1, 020 7833 8336

Farringdon, Angel

Moro is located appropriately on Exmouth Market, between *The Guardian* newspaper and Sadler's Wells Theatre. It's the sort of place you'd expect to see a left-of-centre journalist dining with the tempestuous star of *Carmen*. Moro is run by a married couple, both of whom are called Sam Clarke (though the masculine Sam has no "e" in his surname, like his grandfather, the art historian, Kenneth Clark). Grandpa is best remembered these days for his television series, *Civilization*, which was long marinated in the Mediterranean. Moro is also steeped in Mediterranean culture, in particular that of Andalucia, where the cuisines of southern Europe and North Africa create a delicious synthesis; last time I ate there I started with quail in flatbread with pistachio sauce, followed it with wood roasted *peri-peri* chicken with coriander rice and rocket salad, and concluded with fresh raspberries on a bed of Jerez cream.

As you eat you can watch the chefs at work in the open kitchen at the far end of the restaurant. Finally, I must declare an interest; my girlfriend's son is one of them.

CLIVE SINCLAIR
Novelist

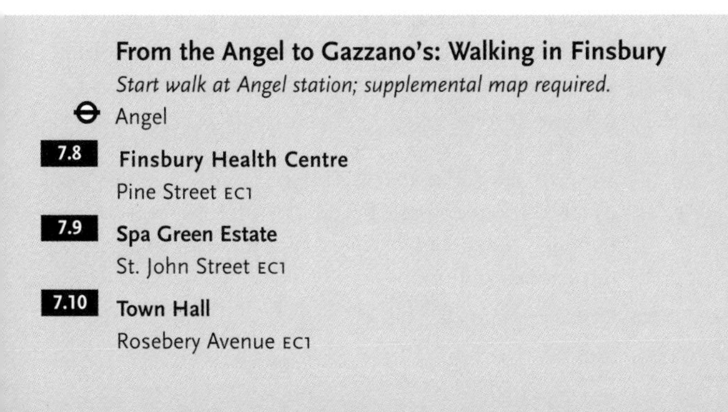

From the Angel to Gazzano's: Walking in Finsbury

Start walk at Angel station; supplemental map required.

Angel

7.8 **Finsbury Health Centre**
Pine Street EC1

7.9 **Spa Green Estate**
St. John Street EC1

7.10 **Town Hall**
Rosebery Avenue EC1

7.11 **Sadler's Wells Theatre**
Rosebery Avenue EC1, ☎ 020 7863 8198

7.12 **Family Records Centre**
1 Myddleton Street EC1, ☎ 020 8392 5300

7.13 **London Metropolitan Archives**
40 Northampton Road EC1, ☎ 020 7332 3820

7.14 **Church of the Holy Redeemer**
24 Exmouth Market EC1

7.15 **Quality Chop House**
94 Farringdon Road EC1, ☎ 020 7837 5093

7.16 **Gazzano's**
169 Farringdon Road EC1, ☎ 020 7837 1586

I never tire of the streets, parks, gardens and squares off Rosebery Avenue. This is northwest Finsbury, a tiny former London borough between the City and the Angel, swallowed by Islington in the sixties and now vanishing for good under the vigorous revival of its medieval name, Clerkenwell. Finsbury is a monument to hands-on local government and pride. "Nothing is too good for ordinary people," declared Berthold Lubetkin, Tbilisi-born architect of the luminous Finsbury Health Centre (1938) and the Spa Green Estate (1950), and councillors agreed. They replaced the blitzed streets with blocks of flats and gardens that have the fresh, open feel of 1950s Berlin to them. Earlier, Finsbury Council treated itself to a sassy Renaissance Town Hall (1895) which looks like a galleon about to set sail in three different directions. (Inside, it's a Borgia movie.)

There are obvious grown-up reasons for visiting the area: the new Sadler's Wells Theatre, London's international dance-venue, the Family Records Centre and the irresistible London Metropolitan Archives. But these are bedded in the textures and realities of London life: a rose-garden, a charred sports pavilion, bookshops, betting shops, park benches with no backs left, broom trees that dazzle and foam like mimosa in June. The working-class high street of Exmouth Market is being replaced by the culture of Starbucks and Pizza Express, but J. D. Seddon's wonderful Church of the Holy Redeemer (1887)—Lombard Romanesque in banded London brick—survives. Around the corner on Farringdon Road, so do the addictive Quality Chop House and G. Gazzano's Italian grocery. Lunch at the Chop, then stock up at Gazzano's. Return to the Angel via unchanged, late Georgian Amwell Street and handsome Myddelton Square.

MICHAEL RATCLIFFE
Critic and journalist

7.17 Wilmington Square

Finsbury WC1
Angel, Farringdon

Small municipal gardens and squares are often poorly conceived and managed but here in Wilmington Square is an enjoyable piece of urban landscape design with the trees now reaching maturity. It provides a welcome respite to the noise and hardness of the heavily trafficked streets in this inner city area. Its designers must have been part of the highly talented team of the now forgotten borough of Finsbury who created the best municipal housing in London.

ALAN BAXTER
Engineer and urban designer

7.18 Gwynne Place

King's Cross WC1
 King's Cross

There aren't many steps in the streets of London. And this wide flight is a bridge between two eras, linking the raucous King's Cross Road to a quiet 19th-century square. "Plum Pudding Steps," as they were called by children who played on them in the fifties, gave Arnold Bennett the setting for his novel of 1923, *Riceyman Steps*, which points out that "dreadful things were often witnessed in Clerkenwell." Then, small shops clustered around the steps: now they're hidden from the street by the huge and ugly arches of the 1970s Ryan Hotel.

SUSANNAH CLAPP
Critic

7.19 Chapel Market

Off Liverpool Road and Upper Street N1

Angel

Tucked away behind busy Upper Street—a couple of minutes' walk from the Angel tube station—this is one of London's oldest street markets. The word is that the stall holdings are hereditary, held in the family for generations. Certainly in the twenty years that I've known the market the faces have aged but seldom changed. Wheeled wooden stalls flank the long narrow street, offering everything from CDs and track shoes to glitzy earrings and secondhand books. But the central feature is fruit and vegetables—great glowing piles of oranges, lemons, grapefruit, mangoes, pineapples, peaches . . . elegant displays of impeccable cabbages, carrots, lettuces, avocados, fennel . . . Everything you've ever heard of and some that you haven't. The flower stalls are Aladdin's caves, brilliant with great shocks of chrysanthemums, foaming gypsophilia, cornucopias of tulips. And the balloon man wanders through the crowds tethered to a cloud of silver helium hearts and globes like Mary Poppins.

PENELOPE LIVELY
Novelist

Islington Stroll

Angel

7.20 **Colebrooke Cottage**
64 Colebrooke Row

7.21 **55 Colebrooke Row**

7.22 **The Old Queen's Head**
44 Essex Road, 020 7354 9273

A short walk from City Road, through the park that separates Duncan Terrace from Colebrooke Row, takes the dispirited or merely hungry to Regent's Canal in Islington, where it emerges from a 970-yard tunnel. This unexpected oasis from the clattering of local traffic is the perfect sheltered spot for lunch. After a few steps down a bank, convenient benches are placed along the path, overlooked on the far side of the canal, by the backs of the great houses of Noel Road. Once drawn by Sickert who had a studio there, he named his engraving of this view *The Hanging Gardens of Islington*.

Leaving the Canal and walking along Colebrooke Row towards St. Peter's Street, it is easy to imagine the rural scene it was until 1861, where the New River ran before the present road was constructed. In less than a quarter of a mile the river could be crossed by three bridges, from which schoolboys fished. The last house on the left, at 64 Colebrooke Row, is Colebrooke Cottage, once detached and since altered, where Charles Lamb and his sister Mary lived from 1823 to 1827. "Elia," that most amiable of all the Romantics, described this cottage with delight:

". . . a white house; with six good rooms in it; the New River . . . runs. . . close to the foot of the house, and behind is a spacious garden, with vines I assure you . . . You enter without passage into a cheerful dining room . . . and above is a lightsome drawing room, three windows . . . I feel like a great lord, never having had a house before . . . "

A glance across the road and on the upper storey of 55

Colebrooke Row just reveals on brickwork, the faded painted lettering of a 19th-century hostel, stating the terms: "Women only 9d and 1/- per night. 4/6 and 6/- per week" (7p and 5p, 21p and 20p approximately).

A short turn up St. Peter's Street leads left to Essex Road, possibly the dullest street in London, and the location of The Old Queen's Head. A minute's walk from Upper Street, this pub was rebuilt on the site of the original Elizabethan inn, unhappily demolished in 1829. Considered one of the finest examples of domestic period architecture, its magnificent wooden carved fireplace and ceiling were transplanted into its replacement. Quite a feat to try to work out the details of the woodwork, but the subject is Diana and Actaeon, with appropriate decorations, of Venus, Bacchus and Plenty.

GEOFFREY ELBORN
Writer

RECOMMENDED READING

Charles Lamb, 'The Last Essays of Elia' in the *Collected Works of Charles Lamb*, Classic Books, 2000.

E. V. Lucas, ed., *The letters of Charles Lamb, to which are added those of his sister Mary Lamb*, J. M. Dent & Sons, Methuen & Co., 1935. o.p.

7.23 Camden Passage Antiques Market

Off Upper Street N1, a short walk from the Angel station

Angel

Go to Portobello Road Market, if you must, but the real antiques market is at Camden Passage. It is confined to an area known as The Angel. Everything—low-end to high-end, finger jewellery to oak armoires—is on display and for sale. (Some of the best restaurants have back entrances onto the passage or use the front entrances on Upper Street.) Power lunch with Tony Blair and his cronies at Granita, about a ten-minute walk from the market (127 Upper Street, 020 7226 3222).

JAY ANTHONY GACH
Composer

7.24

Steve Hatt's Fishmongers

88–90 Essex Road N1, 020 7226 3963

Angel

Steve Hatt's is surely the best fish shop in London, not only because of the variety and quality of the fish on sale, but because Steve is impressively knowledgeable about all things to do with cooking and eating fish. The mussels are particularly worth a try: excellent value and always juicy.

FELICITY LUNN

Curator and lecturer

George Orwell's London

27B Canonbury Square, Tour information 020 7226 8333 (Not on map)

Angel

For fifteen years now I have taken, in all probability, thousands of people on a tour of part of Islington, that I call "George Orwell's Islington." The walk ends in the communal garden at the rear of the flats in which I live in Canonbury Square, my flat being next door to where the author lived at number 27B, on the third floor. The visitors love the sheer unexpected quiet and peace of the garden; after having seen the plaque at the front of the house, it comes as a pleasant surprise after the noise of the square, along the middle of which runs the A1 into London. The other novelty is the realisation that the walk, in the main, goes through what is today a trendy, upmarket area of London, but which was so downbeat and depressing in the 1940s that Orwell declared the flat to be a slum, and used the area with its post-war gloom and general tattiness, plus the bombed-out areas, as the setting for a great deal of *1984*, in particular for the Proles' area in the novel. Both *Animal Farm* and *1984* were completed and published while Orwell lived here.

PETER POWELL

Tour guide

Northampton Lodge

1810–1820

39A Canonbury Square N1, 020 7704 9522 (Not on map)

Highbury, Islington

Estorick Collection

Opened 1998

This unique, interesting and little-known gallery, housed in Northampton Lodge, a beautiful early 19th-century house in Islington, contains the only collection of Futurist Italian painting in Britain. The work on show in the museum/gallery is exclusively by Italian artists, and it includes works by Modigliani, De Chirico, Balla and Severini. The collection was formed by Eric Estorick (1913–1993), an American political scientist and art dealer.

LUCRETIA STEWART
Writer and journalist

Highbury Tennis Centre

Highbury Place N5, 020 7527 4971 (Not on map)

Highbury, Islington

There are few good or accessible courts on which you can get a game near the centre of town. One exception is the Highbury Tennis Centre, at the north end of Highbury Fields. You can usually just turn up to play in surroundings of some Georgian grandeur (*Four Weddings and a Funeral* was filmed over the road) and among the towering sycamores of one of London's most atmospheric small parks. Afterwards, walk across the Fields to Upper Street which has, in the last five years, become lined with cafes. The trend for good eating here was started with the arrival of Casale Franco (137 Upper Street, 020 7226 8994), tucked away in an alley by an old Citroën garage. Good Italian country cooking, and great pizzas.

TIM ADAMS
Writer and editor

THE CITY

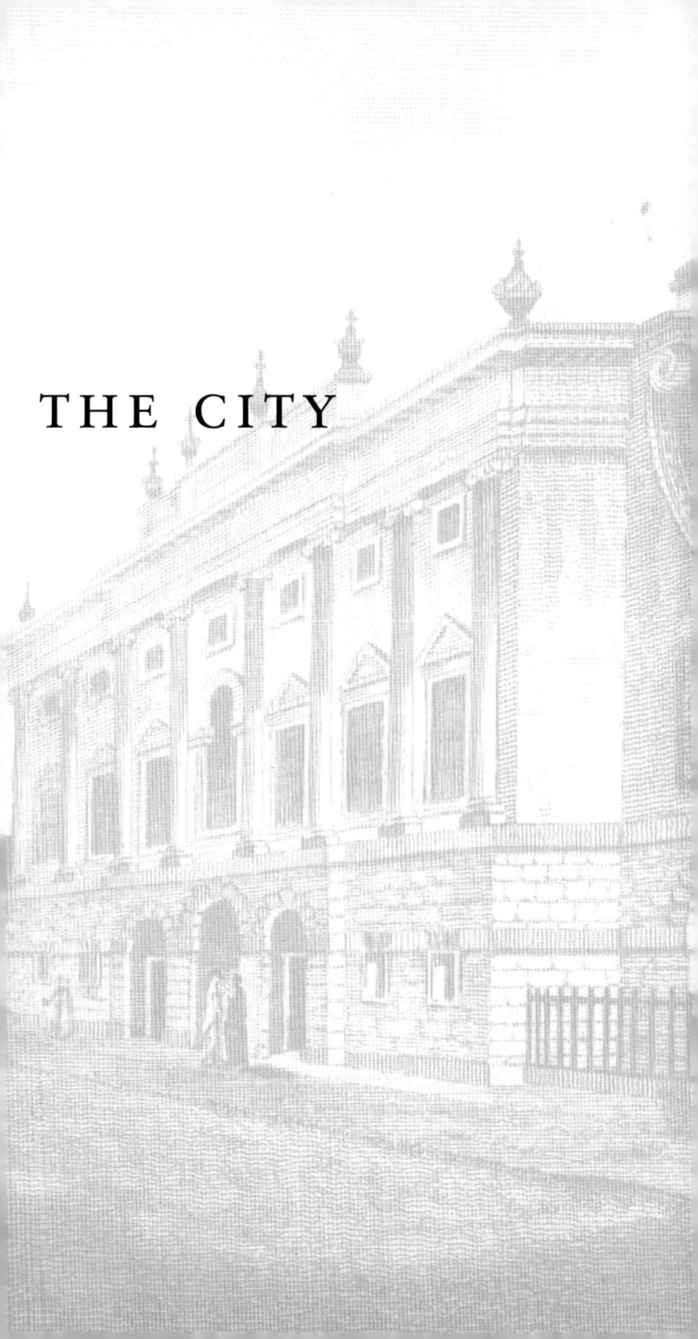

THE CITY

1 St. Paul's Cathedral
2 The Black Friar Pub
3 The former Daily Express Building
4 Inner Temple
5 Middle Temple
6 Temple Church
7 C. Hoare and Co.
8 Prince Henry's Room
9 Lincoln's Inn
10 Gray's Inn
11 The Jerusalem Tavern
12 St. Bartholomew-the-Great Chu

13 Postman's Park
14 Carnevale
15 Bunhill Fields
16 The Barbican
17 St. Botolph's
18 St. Magnus the Martyr
19 Leadenhall Market
20 St. Mary Abchurch
21 St. Mary Wollnoth
22 Bank of England Museum
23 No. 1 Poultry
24 The Corner of Wood Street and Cheapside

THE CITY

8.1 St. Paul's Cathedral

Ludgate Hill EC4, ☎ 020 7236 4128
⊖ St. Paul's

The Monument of Turner
1851–1859, Patrick MacDowell
South Transept

St. Paul's is a great work of theatre in itself. I recommend attending either an evensong to enjoy the choral music or a Sunday Eucharist for the procession. But the great moment of pathos for me is in the south transept where among all the be-medalled and be-weaponed generals and admirals, stands a monument to the painter J. M. W. Turner in a frock coat, holding only a paintbrush.
JEREMY MUSSON
Editor

8.2 The Black Friar Pub

174 Queen Victoria Street EC4, ☎ 020 7236 5474
⊖ Blackfriars

Squeezed in between busy roads and a looming railway bridge, on an awkward corner site by Blackfriars Bridge stands a completely undistinguished Victorian building. Subtle green mosaics and copper signs begin to hint that there may be a better world within.

The interior is an unbelievable collage of richly grained marbles, golden mosaics and copper figures. This is a temple to drinking. Taking inspiration from the friary which stood on this site, the architect, H. Fuller Clark, and sculptors Henry Poole and Frederick Callcott, launched into a decorative frenzy based around a monastic theme. This is the diametric opposite of the Zen monastic aesthetic that has inspired the ubiquitous minimalism of London's fashion boutiques and top-end hotels; this is monastic maximalism.

Art Nouveau and Arts and Crafts details are mixed in to stew with Byzantine and Olde English styles. Every surface is richly grained, decorated or embellished. The pub is at its liveliest on weekday lunchtimes and just after work when it is heaving with sweaty suits while the grotto (carved out of a railway arch) boasts a smoky, booze-soaked atmosphere which could be distilled and sold as essence of London. In fact this whole incredible interior, which was executed in the years between 1905 and 1921, is virtually a distillation of the density, cosiness and womb-like comfort of the very notion of London pub-ness.

EDWIN HEATHCOTE
Architect and writer

8.3 The former Daily Express Building

120 Fleet Street EC4, 020 7774 1000
Blackfriars, St. Paul's

Behind London's façades are wonderfully opulent interiors but, with tight security these days, the only way to get into a building like this—a remarkable Art Deco space now owned by Goldman Sachs—is to join one of the specialist societies which can obtain entrée. The Decorative Arts Society, for example, can be contacted via The Fine Art Society at 148 New Bond Street (020 7629 5116), a unique firm of art dealers established in 1876 and still in the building they commissioned. In their atmospheric galleries they pioneered shows of Whistler, John Singer Sargent, Brangwyn and Sickert. This is one of the best free shows in the West End, with regular exhibitions of paintings, sculpture, ceramics, and modernist design.

MICHAEL BARKER
Designer, author and publisher

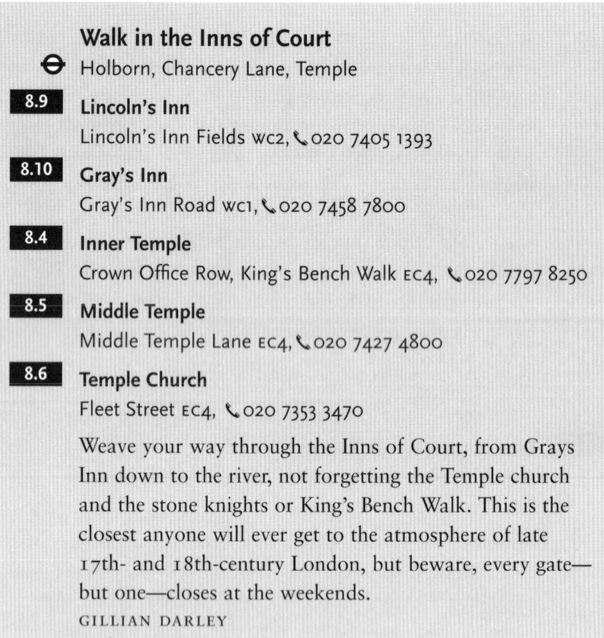

Walk in the Inns of Court

Holborn, Chancery Lane, Temple

8.9 **Lincoln's Inn**
Lincoln's Inn Fields WC2, 020 7405 1393

8.10 **Gray's Inn**
Gray's Inn Road WC1, 020 7458 7800

8.4 **Inner Temple**
Crown Office Row, King's Bench Walk EC4, 020 7797 8250

8.5 **Middle Temple**
Middle Temple Lane EC4, 020 7427 4800

8.6 **Temple Church**
Fleet Street EC4, 020 7353 3470

Weave your way through the Inns of Court, from Grays Inn down to the river, not forgetting the Temple church and the stone knights or King's Bench Walk. This is the closest anyone will ever get to the atmosphere of late 17th- and 18th-century London, but beware, every gate—but one—closes at the weekends.

GILLIAN DARLEY
Architectural writer

8.5 Middle Temple Hall

1562–1573
Middle Temple Lane EC4, 020 7427 4800
Temple

The only building surviving from Shakespeare's time where it is known that one of his plays had its first night: *Twelfth Night*, on 2nd February 1602. With its magnificent double hammer-beam roof, its only rival when it was constructed between 1562 and 1573 was Westminster Hall. Many talented young poets and playwrights, including John Webster, John Ford and John Marston, were students at the Middle Temple and would have dined and argued legal niceties in the Hall. It was a monument to the success of the legal profession. Its function is unchanged today.

GILES DE LA MARE
Publisher

8.7 C. Hoare and Co.

Current building dates to early 1820s; bank established in 1672
37 Fleet Street EC4, 020 7353 4522
Blackfriar's, Chancery Lane, Temple

Messrs. C. Hoare and Co., the oldest bank in Britain, older than the Bank of England, has been owned and run by the Hoare family for nearly four hundred years at 37 Fleet Street. The counters are still of human dimension, behind which real people sit, the messengers and doormen wear top hats, and there is a museum upstairs. It defies the modern age.

BRIAN MASTERS
Author

8.8 Prince Henry's Room

17 Fleet Street EC4, 020 7936 2710
Temple, Chancery Lane

In 1610, the Inner Temple Gate and the house above it were rebuilt. Despite alterations and refurbishments over the centuries, the building is one of the few remaining timber-framed buildings in London, housing some equally remarkable survivals in its interior.

Part of the new building of 1610 continued in use as a tavern under the sign "The Prince's Arms," and the splendid first-floor room (now known, misleadingly, as "Prince Henry's Room") contains: Jacobean oak panelling on its west wall, the rest of the panelling being of 18th-century pine; stained glass windows commemorating the rescue of the building from demolition in 1906 by London County Council, and a wonderful lime plaster ceiling, typical of London decorative plasterwork of 1610. The layout of the enriched ribs of the ceiling is unique among recorded examples, but many of the motifs, cast from wooden moulds, could have been seen in contemporary London houses. At the centre of the ceiling, in a star-shaped field, the Prince of Wales's feathers are flanked by the initials P. H.

Prince Henry (1594–1612) was James I's eldest son and the most popular member of the royal family. His creation as Prince of Wales in 1610 was an occasion of great public celebration. Even if the earlier inn on the site had not been called "The Prince's Arms," it was an appropriate moment for a citizen who did not himself bear arms to mark his loyalty and devotion by displaying the Prince's initials and badge of feather so prominently.

CLAIRE GAPPER
Architectural historian

City of London Afternoon

8.14 **Carnevale**
135 Whitecross Street EC1, 020 7250 3452

8.15 **Bunhill Fields**
(see opposite)

An ideal Saturday afternoon: A stroll through the City of London—virtually a ghost town on this day of the week and preceded or followed by a visit to Carnevale, the vegetarian restaurant and deli in Whitecross Street. If the weather is fine, buy a "take-out" from the deli and proceed to Bunhill Fields, three minutes' walk away, a fine historic graveyard containing the tombs of Bunyan, Thomas Strothard and William Blake. Enjoy your picnic on the central lawns, listening to numerous species of birds but few humans. Otherwise, indulge in a delicious meal in Carnevale's restaurant—a treat is in store!

IMOGEN MAGNUS
Writer and researcher

8.15 Bunhill Fields

Off City Road, entrance on Bunhill Row EC1

Old Street

There are more people buried here than the current population of Southampton (England, that is), partly due to the fact of it having been a plague pit. In 1708 the Calvinist mystics the Camisards gathered here to wait for their leader, Dr Emms, to rise from the dead five months after his interment. Dr Emms disappointed them. But here too are the great Non-Conformists: John Wesley, who lived across the road and whose ghost is still said to visit his grave. Daniel Defoe (1731), John Bunyan (1688), and William Blake (1827), whose gravestone is often decorated by pebbles, in the Jewish tradition, and cut flowers, in the English tradition.

Tumbledown memorials and full grown London plane trees give the place a Gothic air, a mysterious escape from the heaving throb of the City and its financial pulse that surrounds this green remnant. You can still feel the old town here, beneath your feet; even the paths are made from old gravestones. My parish priest regards this place as his personal garden. He is not the only black-garbed figure to haunt its dark green lawns. Take a copy of Peter Ackroyd's *Blake* or his novel *Hawksmoor* and contemplate the launch, in 1796, of M. Lunardi's hot-air balloon from the neighbouring Artillery Fields, his miraculous ascent giving, for the first time, a view of London from the sky.

PHILIP HOARE

Writer, curator and presenter

RECOMMENDED READING

Peter Ackroyd, *Blake*, reissue, Minerva, 1996.

Peter Ackroyd, *Hawksmoor*, Penguin UK, 1993.

Lies next to the Honourable Artillery Company which offers a glimpse of the open meadows that this area (known as "Moorfields") once was. This area exemplifies much that is modern day London: new high rise office buildings of very modern design, squeezing in low income subsidised housing, old fashioned pubs, the Barbican Arts Centre (and its high income tower blocks!), noisy and congested roads . . . Yet Bunhill remains unobservant and indifferent to modern day London. It's a quiet oasis for reflection and repose.

JAY ANTHONY GACH
Composer

City Stroll

⊖ Monument

8.18 **St. Magnus the Martyr**
Lower Thames Street EC3, 020 7626 4481

8.17 **St. Botolph's**
Bishopsgate EC2, 020 7588 3388

Just follow your nose, ear, eye from Monument to Liverpool Street station taking as many twists and turns as you can via Lombard Street, Bishop's Gate, Finsbury Circus—churches, pubs, passages, gardens, monuments, citygoers at work and pleasure. Best done in the week but a certain ghostly splendour at weekend. Organ recitals at St. Magnus the Martyr, St. Botolph's and many others. This is real London.

PIERS PLOWRIGHT
Radio producer

8.16 The Barbican

Silk Street EC2, 020 7588 3008; Arts Centre tel. 020 7638 4141 or 020 7638 8891

⊖ Barbican

Supper at the Barbican—another modern architectural *tour de force* coming back into fashion—followed by a play or concert at the Barbican Arts Centre currently on an artistic "high." The most exciting and imaginative cultural programme in London is found in London's most extraordinary inner city council estate.

JOHN M. ASHWORTH
Chairman, British Library Board

From Leadenhall to Jerusalem

Monument, Bank

8.19 **Leadenhall Market**
Whittington Avenue EC3, off Gracechurch Street

8.13 **Postman's Park**
King Edward Street EC1

8.12 **St. Bartholomew-the-Great Church**
West Smithfield EC1, 020 7606 5171

8.11 **The Jerusalem Tavern**
55 Britton Street EC1, 022 7490 4281

Another magical city walk: coffee in the spectacular Leadenhall Market, then a stroll to the Postman's Park, near St. Paul's, where acts of valour are recorded on a wall of tiles. Even greater spiritual uplift follows in a walk to St. Bartholomew-the-Great Church, ancient and beautiful and strangely friendly, then finally a walk through Smithfield Market to the magic little pub The Jerusalem Tavern for excellent beer.

DEBORAH MOGGACH
Writer

8.20

St. Mary Abchurch

1681–1686, Christopher Wren
Abchurch Lane EC4, 020 7626 0306
Cannon Street, Bank

Simply the warmest and sunniest, and in some ways the most Mediterranean of all the Wren churches, red-brick and homely on the outside, but a great painted dome on the inside, plus quantities of woodwork by Grinling Gibbons and others. And not a tourist ever finds it.

ROGER WOODLEY
Architectural historian

RECOMMENDED READING
Paul Jeffrey, *The Parish Churches of Sir Christopher Wren*, Hambledon and London, Ltd., 1996.
Simon Bradley and Nikolaus Pevsner, *The Buildings of England, London 1: The City of London*, Penguin, 1997.

8.21

St. Mary Woolnoth

1716–1727, Nicholas Hawksmoor
Lombard Street EC3
⊖ Bank

On the prow end of Lombard Street at Bank stands this curious, often overlooked masterpiece. Hawksmoor played with variations of the centralised church plan in his four churches as a response to urban context; at St. Mary the building is jammed on the site, but the Lombard Street elevation with "baroque and roll" windows turns elegantly to the front entrance, and the extraordinary front is stretched between the flank corners by seemingly elastic stone rustication. Then across the street into Sir James Stirling/Michael Wilford's referential post-modern icon No. 1 Poultry (see below). Climb to the roof garden and look back down over St. Mary from a perspective that Hawksmoor could only imagine.

ROBERT DYE
Architect

Church Strolls

Tramp the City with the paperback *London: The City Churches* by Simon Bradley and Nikolaus Pevsner and see as many of Wren's masterpieces (others too) as you have stamina for. When flagging, follow your nose into pubs—

or the many excellent restaurants round Smithfield, now one of London's centres of good eating.

PETER CARSON
Publishing editor and translator from Russian

RECOMMENDED READING
Simon Bradley and Nikolaus Pevsner, *London: The City Churches*, Penguin UK, 1998.

8.22 Bank of England Museum

Museum opened in 1988; the bank has been on this site since 1734, but the present building was built in 1925–1934 by Sir Herbert Baker

Bartholomew Lane EC2, ☎ 020 7601 5545

⊖ Bank

I love wandering around the City of London—and discovering its secret museums, like the wonderful Bank of England Museum in Bartholomew Lane. It's free, and fascinating—a comprehensive history of the Bank and banking. Even if you think you're not interested in finance, you'll love it—it's history, politics and sociology, too.

ERICA WAGNER
Editor

8.23 No. 1 Poultry

1997, James Stirling, Michael Wilford and Associates

1 Poultry EC2

⊖ Bank

One of my favourite buildings is No. 1 Poultry, which was my husband Jim's [Sir James Stirling] penultimate building and his only one in the City of London. As the site was occupied by Mappin and Webb, a Grade II building, marathon court cases ensued, but a development, mainly offices, designed in the mid-eighties for Peter Palumbo, was at last completed in the nineties. The site itself is of great interest. Early Roman wooden buildings with stone extensions were uncovered: some had mosaic floors.

🍴🍷 The restaurant at the top of the building (Le Coq d'Argent, ☎ 020 7395 5000) is the Conran flagship in the City, and is usually full of young, energetic and noisy City traders. But once you are at the top of the building and in the rotunda you could almost be in Italy. Through the gates, the formal parterre with its magnificent views over London (Lutyens' Midland Bank, the Mansion House and Hawksmoor's church) is stunning, the view spoilt only by brash new buildings (not sure whose, but not including Richard Rogers's) towards the river.

LADY STIRLING (AKA MARY SHAND)
Designer

8.24 The Corner of Wood Street and Cheapside

An early winter dusk; bruised light;
what might be snow, except the heat
of London means it's only rain;
the plane trees sharpening the street

cold clotted grey, without a leaf.
Here Wordsworth came in '99
and heard a thrush unloose its song,
so stopped, and took it as a sign

of city-sadness. I press on.
I live in this; it's all mine now;
the silent branch above me and
the load of what cannot be snow.

ANDREW MOTION
Poet Laureate

THE SOUTH BANK

THE SOUTH BANK

1 Imperial War Museum
2 The Museum of Garden History
3 South Bank Stroll
4 Marriott Hotel County Hall Restaurant
5 The Millenium Wheel
6 Hungerford Arches
7 Royal National Theatre
8 Gourmet Pizza Company
9 Oxo Tower

🍴🍷 🎁 10 Tate Modern

11 Shakespeare's Globe Theatre

THE SOUTH BANK

9.1 Imperial War Museum

Lambeth Road SE1, 020 7416 5000

Lambeth North, Elephant & Castle

Hardly a secret, but a place largely ignored by people whose kneejerks are alerted by all three words in the title. Since the British have grown so selectively vague about their own history—never mind anyone else's—and long since passed up the chance for a grown-up Museum of the British Empire on Hyde Park Corner, this is the only world-class historical museum in England. In recording the experience of 20th-century human conflict, its brief is to be both scholarly and popular, educational and entertaining, and it is hard to imagine it better, or more movingly, done. The range of presentation-methods is one of its most striking features, from the pop Trench and Blitz "experiences" to the meticulous curating of personal memorabilia and major war paintings by Sargent, Stanley Spencer, Edward Ardizzone, John Piper and Paul Nash. A tall atrium displays the dinosaurs of war—Spitfire, Mustang, doodlebug, V2 rocket, Monty's tank-like creatures in a museum of natural history. Temporary shows are scrupulously well focused and extend with wit and imagination the idea of war's aftermath—Christian Dior's "New Look," for example, in 1947.

The permanent Holocaust Exhibition, long overdue in Britain, is outstanding, and should be allowed at least two hours, preferably three. (Entry is by timed ticketing, and children discouraged.) Again, diversity of communication keeps the brain keen and open to shock: maps, charts, home movies; a neat, copper-plate ledger of executions, a sewer grid from Lodz; a glaring, bone-white model of Auschwitz under snow. The remorseless industrialisation of mass murder—backed by hard evidence acquired, or loaned, from Germany, Poland and the Ukraine—is both tempered and made more painful by the filmed witness of surviving British Jews.

MICHAEL RATCLIFFE
Critic and journalist

9.2 The Museum of Garden History

Lambeth Palace Road SE1, 020 7401 8865
Lambeth, Westminster

The Knot Garden
Designed for the Museum in 1983
Located in the 14th-century churchyard

The Knot Garden is an oasis of calm in one of the busiest parts of London. It was created out of the churchyard of St. Mary's Lambeth (1370, restored 1851), now the Museum of Garden History. It contains the fine Tradescant Sarcophagus. John Tradescant was gardener to Charles I and the knot garden is planted with flowers of that period. St. Mary's is next to Lambeth Palace, which is off Lambeth Palace Road. To find the Knot Garden you walk through the museum, which in itself is interesting, and where you can have tea.

CLAYRE PERCY
Landmark Trust

9.3 South Bank Stroll

Lambeth North, Westminster

Just to the north of Lambeth Bridge, on the south side of the Thames, join the riverside walk which begins as the Jubilee Walkway and follow it under its various different names, all the way to the Tate Modern at Bankside. The city's most imposing buildings, from Parliament to St. Paul's, unscroll along the opposite bank while the city's coolest people rollerblade past you. If you only have half a day in London, this is the way to use it.

LUCY HUGHES-HALLETT
Writer

9.4 Marriott Hotel County Hall Restaurant

Westminster Bridge Road SE1, 020 7928 5200
Waterloo, Westminster

The best view of the Houses of Parliament at sunset is from across the river, from the County Hall Restaurant of the Marriott Hotel, with its generous oak lined spaces left over from when this building was the London County Council's grand floor. The entrance is equally grand, being the old Council Members' entrance. Close-up, the London Eye, my favourite Millennium structure, slowly turns.

LADY STIRLING (AKA MARY SHAND)
Designer

9.5 The Millennium Wheel / London Eye

2000, David Marks and Julia Barfield
Jubilee Gardens SE1, next to County Hall; 0870 500 0600
Waterloo, Westminster

Is it art? Architecture? A feat of engineering? Who cares. The Millennium Wheel—or the London Eye (so good they named it twice)—is the most compelling spectacle on the London skyline since the Crystal Palace caught fire. The best way to see it is by accident—maybe innocently glancing up from your tourist map as you step onto Westminster Bridge, the whole sunlit upturned bicycle wheel of it in the sky, the spokes just about turning as if momentarily abandoned by a giant ten-year-old gone to get his dad to fix the chain back on; or perhaps just an arc's gleam of its hugeness curving over Hungerford Bridge as you exit the Embankment Tube; or looming sudden and impossibly tall as you round Jubilee Gardens, taking your eyes by surprise. Try not to laugh out loud.

And then look up at it from directly below, the 32 Brobdingnagian glass lozenges and steely white whatnots and cables and zigzagging girders, and then right up there—450 feet from the ground—those tiny faces at the windows, their features indistinct, looking down at you. And this is before you part with any money. . . .

It may look like a fairground attraction, but the ride is not the point. The ascent, fittingly, is as slow as the turn of a century—no thrills, no spills, no one throwing up; the only sounds the hum of the air-conditioning and the clunk of jaws being dropped as you hit the summit. Apparently, on a clear day, you might spot St. Albans Cathedral 25 miles away—though for most of us, the idea even of seeing Nelson's Column from Waterloo without the aid of an aeroplane seems fanciful enough. To those of us unused to skyscraping vistas, the panorama turns the familiar into something strange like a trick from modern art—an East Enders river scything a bend into a London of Lego bridges, Dinky double deckers, a toytown Parliament, glassy water-front blocks cut down to size, a paperweight St. Paul's, Hornby trains; the concrete hutches of the South Bank along to the Tate Modern and the Globe at Southwark—Shakespeare's "wooden O." I wonder what he would have made of this metal one.

PHIL HOGAN

Columnist and novelist

A Summer Afternoon

⊖ Waterloo

9.5 **Millennium Wheel / London Eye**

(see opposite)

9.8 **Gourmet Pizza Company**

56 Upper Ground SE1, 020 7928 318

A ride on the London Eye and then a stroll up river in early evening in the summer. The river walk has become a magnet for street entertainment and personally my biggest buzz was looking down on the fire eaters from the top of the wheel. A pizza at Gourmet Pizza Company in Gabriel's Wharf is fun too.

KAREN WRIGHT

Editor

9.6

Hungerford Arches

158 Concert Hall Approach SE1, 020 7928 3405
Waterloo

A Memoir of the Century

1967 until 1989 (the year of Topolski's death), never formally completed; Feliks Topolski

The Topolski Century, housed unpromisingly in a railway arch on London's South Bank, is the city's only permanent exhibition devoted to a single art work. Vibrant and violent, this expressionist collage chronicling the glories and horrors of the 20th century displays all the decadence and cruelty of a canvas by Dix. Part maze, part stage set, pure art, it gains added drama from the trains rolling towards Charing Cross Station overhead. Every visitor to the National Theatre or Royal Festival Hall should allow time to experience Feliks Topolski's unique vision.

MICHAEL ARDITTI
Novelist

9.7

Royal National Theatre

Sir Denys Lasdun and Partners, 1967–77
South Bank Centre SE1, 020 7452 3000
Waterloo, Embankment

Go to the National Theatre. No need to buy a ticket. Theatre is all around you in Denys Lasdun's masterpiece of 20th-century public architecture. To appreciate it properly you need to go alone. Buy a playscript from the bookshop, preferably Stoppard. Find a comfortable seat high up in the building giving you wonderful vistas down the Thames. Hear the distant hum of action, the clash of Shakespearian sword fights, from the auditoria. Watch the ebb and flow of people entering and exiting these grand convivial spaces. Patronize the bars and restaurants when the crowds vacate them. Spend a late afternoon there and stay on into the night.

FIONA MACCARTHY
Biographer and critic

9.9 Oxo Tower

Barge House Street SE1

Waterloo, Blackfriars

Walking east along the Thames from the concrete brutalism of the South Bank Centre, I have a habit of visiting the unique contemporary retail design studios in the Oxo Tower and having a quick drink and a bite to eat at its panoramic brasserie. Despite the huge neon "OXO" beacon that radiates from the tower it is not the easiest place to find. Once there, though, the views from the eighth floor are spectacular, from St. Paul's, along the Thames, to the Houses of Parliament. What's more you don't have to eat there, to appreciate them. Although there is a restaurant, bar and brasserie (owned by Harvey Nichols, 020 7803 3888) there is also a free public viewing gallery.

ELLIOT BOYD

Architect

9.10 Tate Modern

2000, Herzog and de Meuron

Bankside SE1, 020 7887 8000

Southwark, Blackfriars, Mansion House, London Bridge

The new museum for international contemporary art is one of the city's least-kept secrets. Ever since it opened at Bankside in May 2000, Londoners have been bragging about it almost non-stop. And it really is spectacular: Swiss architects Herzog and de Meuron have converted, with grandeur and elegance, a post-war power station designed by Giles Gilbert Scott, the man responsible for, amongst other things, the classic red telephone box.

The idea behind the new museum was to create enough space to house the Tate Gallery's extensive collection (most of its British art is still on show at the original Tate on Millbank), but the experience remains a predominantly architectural one. The entrance to the main turbine hall is breathtaking—so much so that the gigantic Louise

Bourgeois sculptures in the centre (commissioned for the opening and a temporary show) seem like furniture for this enormous living room. The architectural details are so beautiful that the art often seems a secondary decoration. The escalators, the wood panels on the stairs or the glowing boxes of light are more likely to attract attention. Away from the main hall, many of the galleries are small. This works extremely well in some cases, such as the Surrealist room, painted a shocking pink and populated by the crawling, obsessive works of the period. In other cases, you simply feel underwhelmed—a monumental Richard Long, for example, looks lost and cramped in a corner.

But there are always a number of pleasant surprises. The watercolour nudes of Marlene Dumas (in the room next to the Francis Bacons) are quietly intriguing, as is the series of boxes that makes up Susan Hiller's excellent *From the Freud Museum* (next to the Surrealists).

As for the rest of the building, it's worth knowing that the bookshop is the best in the city for art and photography, by quite a long way, and has a good selection of books about film. Above all, don't leave without taking in the view from the cafe at the top: St. Paul's Cathedral looms large across the river, and all of London seems to spread out before you.

GABY WOOD
Writer

9.11 Shakespeare's Globe Theatre

Completed in 1997, Pentagram Design Ltd. Modelled on the design of the original Globe Theatre, whose first recorded performance was in 1599.

New Globe Walk SE1, 020 7902 1500

Southwark, Mansion House, London Bridge

Fact: theatre is better in London. Don't argue. It's true. They take it more seriously, young people go, and despite the protestations from artists that it is under-funded, the government gives the institutions buckets of money. The most astonishing theatrical experience takes place at the Globe, a recreation of Shakespeare's playhouse, the "Wooden O" itself. What initially seemed to the *cognoscenti* (or "luvvies" as they're called over here) a potentially Disney-fied experience has proven the opposite. To hear an actor deliver a soliloquy directly to the Groundlings from a bare stage with only the sun for illumination redefines Shakespeare; in fact, it redefines theatre in general. It almost makes any theatrical innovation since 1595 seem obsolete and twee. Who needs scenery, lighting, helicopters, when you can connect, one on one, with the most glorious poetry ever written? Granted, not every actor is great, not every production is flawless, but, as a rule, these are life-changing experiences. Especially for a theatregoer.

GLEN ROVEN
Composer

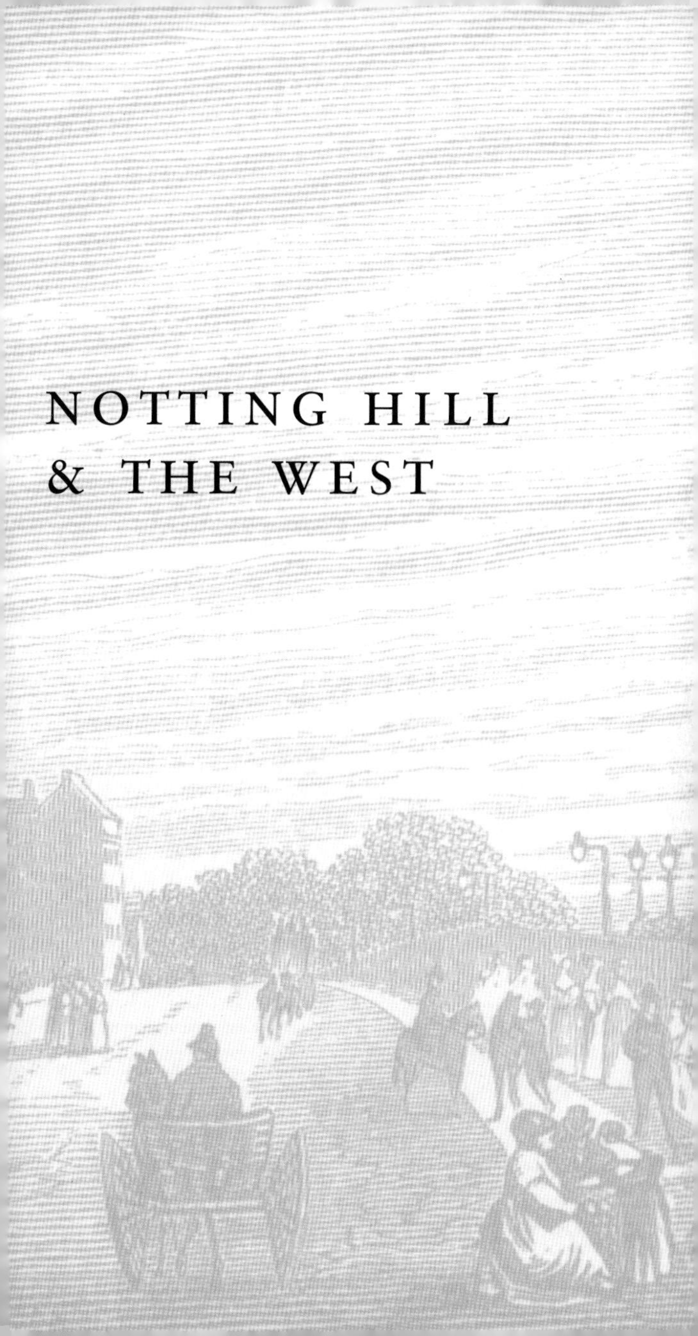

NOTTING HILL & THE WEST

10
Kensal Green Cemetery
25
Harrow Road
Grand Union Canal
Wormwood
Scrubs
24
Wood Lane
Wornington Road
10
11
Golborne
Portobello Road
9
St. Quintin Avenue
St Mark's Road
Westway
8
Ladbroke
Grove
Lancaster Road
Ladbroke Grove
Artillery
Lane
Du Cane Road
6
7
Westway (A40)
Bramley Road
Latimer
Road
Elgin Crescent
White City
Wood Lane
West Cross Route
Notting
Hill
Bloemfontein Road
1
Clarendon Road
Pottery Lane
2
Shepherd's
Bush
Uxbridge Road
Holland Park Avenue
Holland Par
Shepherd's
Bush
Coningham Road
Shepherd's
Bush Garden
Holland Road
Addison Road
Goldhawk
Road
Goldhawk Road
17
Askew Rd.
Shepherd's Bush Rd.
Addison Road
Kensington
Olympia
Holland
Road
Ravenscourt
Park
Askew Rd.
Goldhawk Road
Ravenscourt
Park
Glenthorne Road
Hammersmith
North End Road
Hammersmith Road
Great West Road
Talgarth Road
Hammersmith
Bridge Road
Queen Caroline
Street
Baron's Court
West
Kensington
River Thames
23

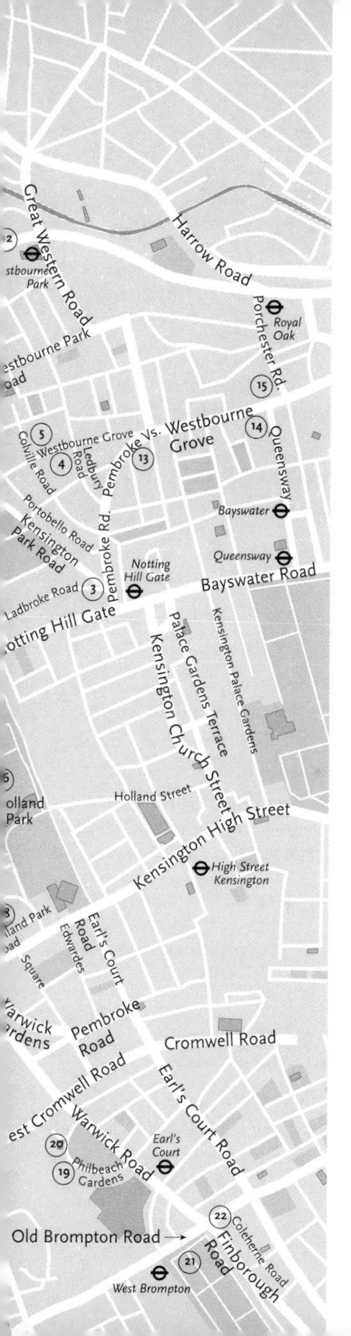

NOTTING HILL & THE WEST

1 St. Francis Church
2 6 Clarendon Road
3 Aurum
4 Wild at Heart
5 Tom Conran's
6 Graham & Greene
7 Mr Christian's Delicatessan & Wines
8 Café Grove
9 Emma Bernhardt
10 Olowu Golding
11 Lisboa Patisserie
12 The Westway
13 Westbourne Grove
14 Fresco
15 Porchester Centre Baths
16 Japanese Garden
17 The Peacock House
18 Leighton House
19 The Ashdel Centre
20 St. Cuthbert's Church
21 Brompton Cemetery
22 The Troubadour
23 The Gate
24 Wormwood Scrubs
25 Kensal Green Cemetery

NOTTING HILL & THE WEST

10.1 St. Francis Church

1859–1860, Henry Clutton; additions, 1861–1863, John Francis Bentley

Pottery Lane W11, ☎ 020 7227 7968

⊖ Holland Park

This is the first public building (neo-Gothic Arts and Crafts movement) built by John Francis Bentley, the first Catholic architect in the Post-Reformation England. He later built Westminster Cathedral.

AL ORENSANZ

Director, Angel Orensanz Foundation

10.2 6 Clarendon Road

6 Clarendon Road W11, ☎ 020 7727 3330

⊖ Holland Park

A busy, small neighbourhood restaurant and an Anglo-American venture: limited menu, about four main dishes, but well cooked and often adventurous. A reasonable wine list that has reasonable markups. Most of the materials come from nearby shops. Comfortable, bright, modern interiors, but service inclined to be slow. With a bottle of wine—£30 a head.

A. A. TAIT

Art historian

10.3 Aurum

7 Ladbroke Road W11, ☎ 020 7727 9720

⊖ Notting Hill Gate

London has recently sprouted pavement cafes in abundance, the drawback being in many cases the narrowness of the space available for tables and the nearness of traffic.

Aurum, a restaurant at 7 Ladbroke Road in Notting Hill, has been in the same family for many years. Until recently, the father, who is a Greek Cypriot, ran it under the name Savvas. Now his son has covered the general forecourt with an awning. Hedged with box, set back from noise and fumes, this is a delightful place to watch Notting Hill go by.

EMMA TENNANT
Novelist

Portobello Morning

Notting Hill Gate, Ladbroke Grove

10.8 **Cafe Grove**
253A Portobello Road W11 020 7243 1094

10.6 **Graham & Greene**
4 Elgin Crescent W11, 020 7727 4594

10.9 **Emma Bernhardt**
301 Portobello Road W11, 020 8960 2929

10.10 **Olowu Golding**
367 Portobello Road W11, 020 8960 7570

10.7 **Mr Christian's Delicatessan & Wines**
11 Elgin Crescent W11, 020 7229 0501

10.4 **Wild at Heart**
49A Ledbury Road W11, 020 7727 3095

10.5 **Tom Conran's**
226 Westbourne Grove W11, 020 7221 8818

I bought my flat smack in the middle of Notting Hill at the beginning of the Bosnian War. I needed a peaceful place to return to, to connect with human beings after living in a war zone. A walk down Portobello Road at 9AM on a weekday brings me back to earth. I buy flowers, fresh-ground coffee, sit outside at the Cafe Grove, eating an omelette, reading *The Times*. Then shop—Graham & Greene, Emma Bernhardt, and a stop at the amazing clothes designer Olowu Golding. I visit Mr Christian's on

Elgin Crescent for fresh bread, brownies, cookies, olives and soup. Then walk down Westbourne Grove: I buy flowers at Wild at Heart before meeting friends for the best cappuccino outside Rome at Tom Conran's. Everyone knows each other. The market vendors call out "Hello Darling!" It feels very much like a world within a world.
JANINE DI GIOVANNI
Foreign correspondent, The Times

10.11 Lisboa Patisserie

55 Golborne Road W10, 020 8968 5242
Ladbroke Grove, Westbourne Park

Golborne Road off Portobello is home to Portuguese cafe Lisboa bursting with Portuguese locals and Ladbroke Grove *cognoscenti* devouring custard tarts and other pastries to rival the very best in Lisbon.
LUCINDA MONTEFIORE
Radio producer

10.12 The Westway

The Westway (A40M) stretches between Edgware Road and Ladbroke Grove, leading into the M40 motorway. Rent a car or hire a cab.

London is a city that rarely entered the 20th century, and to find this stretch of motorway little more than a stone's throw from Marble Arch is a poignant reminder of what might have been. Join it by travelling west along the Marylebone Road, not far from 221B Baker Street, Sherlock Holmes's notional address. The Westway is a continuous overpass some three miles in length, running towards White City, home to BBC Television, and then to Shepherd's Bush, where Pissarro's house is still standing.

By international standards the Westway is unremarkable, and affords a view of some of the most dismal housing in London. But that is not its point. Rising above

the crowded 19th-century squares and grim stucco terraces, this massive concrete motion-sculpture is an heroically isolated fragment of the modern city London might once have become. There are few surveillance cameras and you can make your own arrangements with the speed limits. Corbusier remarked that a city built for speed is a city built for success, but the Westway, like Angkor Wat, is a stone dream that will never awake. As you hurtle along this concrete deck you briefly join the 20th century and become a citizen of a virtual city-state borne on a rush of radial tyres.
J. G. BALLARD
Novelist

On the map it looks bizarre: a broad blue flyover bang in the middle of the city speeding from nowhere to nowhere. But if you get the chance to go on it when no one else is about—heading west—there is a rare moment of freedom to be had as you soar up into the sky leaving the long reach of Marylebone behind you, lifting above the steel drums of the Carnival; the road curves offering possibilities unimaginable before falling back inexorably to the small comedies of Sheperds Bush, Ealing and Notting Hill.
ROMESH GUNESEKERA
Author

If you head west at sunset you get the most beautiful urban skyscape.
ALEXANDRA SHULMAN
Editor

10.13 Westbourne Grove

Between Queensway and Kensington Park Road W2
Bayswater, Notting Hill Gate

No one in their right mind reveals their secret, favourite restaurant because then it is no longer a secret and every Tom, Dick and Sally turn up and squeeze you out. But here's a compromise. I reveal Westbourne Grove as the

real heart of London restaurant land. In its half-mile between Queensway and Kensington Park Road, the Grove and its side streets have restaurants representing 21 national cuisines, all good and all eminently affordable. I know. I live in the middle of them and have tried them all.
PHILIP KNIGHTLEY
Writer

10.14 **Fresco**
25 Westbourne Grove W2, 020 7221 2355
Bayswater/Notting Hill Gate

This is not a trendy, state-of-the-art Notting Hill cafe. This is a small, family-run Middle Eastern restaurant open day and night. They serve fresh carrot and ginger juice, Mediterranean *mezze*, hot pita bread—and they have the best *shwarma* outside Beirut. Close your eyes and you're in Jerusalem, Damascus, Cairo . . . Plus, no tourists!
JANINE DI GIOVANNI
Foreign correspondent

Turkish and Russian Baths

10.15 **Porchester Centre Baths**
Queensway W2, 020 7792 2919
Queensway, Bayswater

12.11 **York Hall Baths**
Old Ford Road at the junction of Cambridge Heath Road E2, 020 8980 2243
Bethnal Green

The proliferation of small private health clubs has seen the demise of most of the grand Turkish baths built by local authorities at the beginning of the 20th century. But the little wooden boxes of the sauna cannot rival the pleasures of steaming halls. The Turkish bath at the Porchester Centre is the most magnificent survival. It even uses the old Latin names for the various areas. But if you want a taste of how

things used to be, go to the Russian baths at York Hall in the East End. This has the easy-going camaraderie of a more innocent, agenda-free age. Some gays, mostly straights, but no one cares about that.
DUNCAN FALLOWELL
Author

10.16 Japanese Garden

1991, Chris Churchman, HOM Landscape
Northwest corner of Holland Park
⊖ Holland Park

The proportions of this replica of a Kyoto garden dismiss an accusation of "tweeness" or bonsai look-alike. A waterfall, a low bridge, a fast-growing collection of flowering shrubs and *clematis stellata* make a pleasant enclave raised from the ground and enclosed by walls of huge stones brought from Japan. Known as the "Waabi-Saabi," this is a garden worthy of comparison with the water garden at Lake House, Wiltshire.
EMMA TENNANT
Novelist

10.17 The Peacock House

1905, Halsey Ricardo
8 Addison Road W14
⊖ Holland Park, Kensington (Olympia)

Holland Park is full of splendid town houses built for nouveau toffs, but none is grander or stranger than 8 Addison Road. It was designed in 1905 by Halsey Ricardo. The exterior elevations are sheathed with semi-vitrified glazing bricks; some blue to reflect the sky, others blue-green to echo the surrounding foliage. Within is a neo-Byzantine dome, dreamed up by a pre-Raphaelite with the unlikely name of Gaetano Meo. But an even greater glory are its tiles (to be found both within and without), all the creation of William de Morgan. These were chosen not only for their intrinsic beauty, but because "the finger of time leaves [glazed tiles] obstinate and unaffected." They certainly have lost none of their original vitality. Bathrooms (which all still contain their contemporary fixtures) are populated by creatures extant and extinct, while larger spaces display Orpheus beguiling ferocious beasts with his lute, or the adventures of Jason and the Argonauts. Elsewhere there are quotations from Homer's *Odyssey*.

CLIVE SINCLAIR
Novelist

10.18 Leighton House

1866–1879, George Aitchison
12 Holland Park Road W14, 020 7602 3316
High Street Kensington

The artist Lord Leighton, then at the height of his fame and prosperity, built this handsome mansion, one of a number in this area occupied by wealthy 19th-century artists, as both residence and studio, with the assistance of the architect George Aitchison. Its chief attraction—wonderfully cool on hot summer days—is its Arab Hall, decorated with 13th-17th-century Persian tiles, with a fountain in the centre and damascene stained glass windows. The home also contains some splendid pottery by William de Morgan, also famed in his day as a novelist, and pictures by Leighton and his contemporaries. Holland Park is near at hand.

FRANCIS KING
Novelist and critic

Until modern times, artists did not paint works with the intention of having them displayed in public museums; rather, their destination was usually the private collection of a patron. Rarely can we experience works of art in the kind of domestic context they were intended to adorn. Such an opportunity is provided by Leighton House, the home and studio of Frederick, Lord Leighton (1830–1896). The classical exterior was very unusual for the time (contrast it with Webb's Gothic studio for Val Prinsep next door) and emulated an Italianite villa, reflecting the theme and style of Leighton's own paintings. With Alma-Tadema and Edward Poynter, Leighton set himself to oppose Pre-Raphaelite romantic realism. Many of his paintings, some in his earlier style reminiscent of the Florentine *quattrocento*, others in his later refined pseudo-Hellenistic classicism, are displayed in the house along with his sculpture.

There are numerous inventive details throughout. For example, the window positioned above the fireplace (the flue ingeniously concealed by an S-bend) features a sliding, mirrored shutter affording a view to the garden on the ground floor. What are more evident, however, are the richly colored interiors; the red walls and black woodwork, for example, imitate a Venetian *palazzo*. The house established Aitchison as a master of decoration. In 1877 he added the celebrated Arab Hall, based on the chamber of the 12th-century Islamic Palace of La Zisa at Palermo, to display Leighton's collection of Saracenic tiles. William de Morgan designed new tilework, Boehm carved the capitals and Walter Crane contributed the mosaic frieze. The back door for the models, the generous promenades for the clients, and the luxurious studios are reminders of the successful artist's social position in mid-Victorian era. The exuberant ornamentation evokes Oscar Wilde's description of the house and studio of the fashionable artist Basil Hallward in *The Picture of Dorian Gray*.

PETER J. HOLLIDAY
Historian of Classical Art and Archeology

Hidden gem, close to the delight of the most civilised park (Holland Park) in London.

PAUL BAGGALEY
Director, Harvill Press

Two Earl's Court Secrets

⊖ Earl's Court

10.19 **The Adshel Centre**

1990s, Apicella Associates (now Pentagram Design Ltd.); winner of 1991 RIBA award

55 Philbeach Gardens SW5

10.20 **St. Cuthbert's Church**

1884–1888, H. Roumieu Gough

51 Philbeach Gardens SW5, ☎ 020 7835 1389

Down an alley, off a side street, hidden from the Cromwell Road by advertising hoardings, are two extraordinary buildings, all the more extraordinary for being in the aesthetic wasteland of Earl's Court and for their juxtaposition. Adshel, the street-furniture people, have created a site that belongs on *The Truman Show*: an elegant glass workspace surrounded by a pristine plaza, where they showcase their wares. Planning committees come from around the world to marvel at the marketing men's vision of the future: pay-as-you-go bicycles; bus shelters that double as computerised information-points; public lavatories with cash dispensers built in. Security has been tightened recently, but you should be able to sneak a look during office hours.

The church itself is only unlocked for worship—Wednesdays and Fridays at 6:30pm and Sundays at 11am, but the doors open an hour early on Sundays. Massive, red-brick, Gothic with traces of Arts and Crafts, it's incredibly high—what the Catholics might have built here had there been no Reformation. Most Italian duomos could offer nothing better in mosaics, marble or Old Masters. There's a Lady Chapel, and a carved rood screen, glinting brass and copper railings and painted Stations of the Cross to rival those in Amsterdam Cathedral. Yet it reeks of the English sensibility, as expressed in the religious revival of the time. So much work went into making this place so beautiful, but congregations are tiny now. They can still afford to pay for a choir, though. So sit a while, smell the incense, and reflect on how the changes of the last hundred years—the Adshel century—have made this treasure so unappreciated. And before you leave, remember to search out the stained glass of the seventh-century St. Cuthbert as a boy, playing golf.

TIM WILLIS
Journalist

RECOMMENDED READING
Simon Jenkins, *England's Thousand Best Churches*, Allen Lane, The Penguin Press, 1999.

Earl's Court Stroll

⊖ Earl's Court

10.21 **Brompton Cemetery**
Between Old Brompton Road and Fulham Road

10.22 **The Troubadour**
265 Old Brompton Road, ☎ 020 7370 1434

Walk to the other end of Philbeach Gardens, endure the thundering Warwick Road for a few minutes, and you arrive at the Old Brompton Road. First, turn right for Brompton Cemetery, a Victorian burial ground with catacombs attached. The Native American chief who died while performing in Buffalo Bill's rodeo at the nearby exhibition centre has been repatriated now, but there's still an extraordinary selection of inhabitants and some outlandish memorials to them.

Explore the side paths where apart from a little trimming, the wildflowers and birdlife have been left to get on with it, to picturesque effect—then return by the main avenue. Here, the colonnades of the necropolis's curving crescents are a favourite for cruising gays, who only approach one another. Besides, it's time for a drink, or a good plain meal, or to catch an act. Go back up the Old Brompton Road for two hundred yards, and you arrive at The Troubadour. Possibly the first cafe in London to be decorated with kitchen and garden bric-a-brac enamel

signs, old Toby jugs and so on, it's probably the last to allow you to dawdle all afternoon over a single coffee while you discuss revolutionary politics to a salsa background. The regular chess gang who hog the window tables are an added attraction, as is the jazz/folk club downstairs. Now home to the likes of Jacques Brel homagiste Philip Keays, the venue was played by Bob Dylan and Paul Simon in the sixties. A word of warning: Madonna was recently seen upstairs at The Troubadour, so it may be getting trendy.
TIM WILLIS
Journalist

10.23 The Gate

51 Queen Caroline Street w6, 020 8748 6932
Hammersmith

Coming out of the Apollo Theatre and confronted by a huge flyover and busy roundabout you could never imagine that just around the corner is one of the most magical courtyards and best vegetarian restaurants in London. Set behind a beautiful iron gate is a tranquil leafy courtyard with stone steps leading up to the first-floor former studio of artist Sir Frank Brangwyn. Now a light-filled restaurant with deep yellow painted walls, it's definitely worth visiting for lunch, or a candlelit evening meal.
ELLIOT BOYD
Architect

10.24 Wormwood Scrubs

North of White City and the Westway, with Scrubs Lane at its east end

East Acton

Wormwood Scrubs is the nearest wild place to central London, with something of heath or moor about it, fringed by rugged copses and brambles. The bleakness is underscored by London's nastiest prison, looking unexpectedly elegant along its south side. But you really are out of it here and can be alone and free, at worst troubled only by the occasional dog, or model plane enthusiast. From the north side—surprisingly high and breezy—is a view which takes in the city's newer wonders—the Crystal Palace radio tower on the Surrey Hills, the Post Office Tower, Canary Wharf Tower and the Millennium Wheel. Here is London's largest sky, usually scudding in from the west.

DUNCAN FALLOWELL
Author

10.25 Kensal Green Cemetery

1833
Harrow Road W10
Kensal Green

Kensal Green was the smartest as well as the earliest of London's great public cemeteries. Normally next to empty—but never creepy—it contains around 250,000 bodies, from Isambard Kingdom Brunel (1859) to Thackeray (1863) and downwards. It is the quintessence of late romanticism: heart-piercing epitaphs, crumbling statuary, a sea of grasses and shaggy trees. All the pomp and vibrancy of Victorian London has ebbed away, leaving this a charnel house of jumbled monuments. To see the tomb of William Mulready the painter, in a November dusk, under its pall of chestnut trees is to come close to a rare sort of bliss—and just off the Harrow Road, too.

ROGER BOWDLER
Historian, English Heritage

Fulham Palace Garden

ca. 1750
Bishop's Avenue just off Fulham Palace Road SW6,
020 7736 2640 (Not on map)
Putney Bridge

When I was checking the view from the site of Mary Shelley's Putney home for a biography I completed this year, I found myself gazing at the walls which enclosed the bishop's palace at Fulham. Crossing the river by what would have been the old timber bridge in her day, I circled the garden wall and wandered through the West Gate to find myself in a gloriously landscaped private garden, shaded by cedars and leading down to what is currently (before restoration) one of London's most enchanting walled gardens, complete with box hedges, delicately collapsing greenhouses in which peaches still smother the walls, and a cloud of yellow butterflies nestling against the red brick. The garden is available for hire for parties through Wandsworth Borough Council.
MIRANDA SEYMOUR
Biographer, novelist and critic

Fulham Football Ground

Stevenage Road SW6 (Not on map)
⊖ Putney Bridge

On the Thames at Putney, lovely walks on the river banks.
ALAN ROSS (1922–2001)
Author and editor

Chiswick House

1727, William Kent, Lord Burlington
Burlington Lane W4, ☎ 020 8995 0508 (Not on map)
⊖ Chiswick

I love Chiswick House as a piece of Palladian Italy marooned in suburban Chiswick. Amid a wasteland of mock Tudor terraced houses stands a fragment of the warm south: a perfect Renaissance design, complete with obelisks, classical statues, formal gardens and a pagan temple. Even in the depths of an English winter it never appears to succumb to the gloom of its surroundings.
WILLIAM DALRYMPLE
Travel writer

RECOMMENDED READING

James Lees-Milne, *Earls of Curation: Five Great Patrons of 18th-Century Art*, Penguin UK, 2001. Toby Barnard and Jane Clark, eds., *Lord Burlington: Architect, Art and Life*, Hambledon and London Ltd., 1994.

Osterley Park

1576, Sir Thomas Gresham; remodelled 1761-1780 by Robert and James Adam

Jersey Road, Isleworth, Middlesex TW7, ☎ 020 8568 7714
(Not on map)
Follow brown tourist signs on A4, towards Gilette Corner, turning up Thornbury Road and Jersey Road to park entrance.
Open 1 April to 31 October, Wednesdays-Sundays, 1pm–4:30pm.
⊖ Osterley

Less than 45 minutes' journey by underground from central London and a fifteen-minute walk will bring you to the most perfectly preserved masterpiece of the Adam Brothers, set in an idyllic park within sound (alas) of Heathrow. Osterley Park, originally built as a country seat for the Elizabethan tycoon Sir Thomas Gresham in 1576 (the Queen actually slept here that year), was remodelled with supreme elegance for the Georgian bankers Francis and Robert Child in the latest fashionable taste devised by the Adam brothers. Given to the National Trust in 1949, the house retains in unique completeness the original Adam furnished interiors, devised with a flair and panache that caused a sensation in the 1770s. The novel Etruscan Dressing Room, part inspired by Wedgwood and Herculaneum, remains one of the first conscious attempts to create a modern style of interior design. The house also has the dubious distinction of having turned away as visitors Thomas Jefferson and John Adams in 1786 because they had failed to acquire tickets in advance and Mrs Child was at the Newmarket races! Be sure, therefore, to check the opening arrangements.

JOHN WILTON-ELY
Art historian

RECOMMENDED READING
Geoffrey Beard, *The Work of Robert Adam*, John Bartholomew & Son, 1978.
Eileen Harris, *Osterley Park, Middlesex*, Official Guidebook, The National Trust, 1994.

Gunnersbury Park

Gunnersbury Park W5
The park is a five-minute walk from the tube station; buses #E3 and #H91 also stop outside the park. (Not on map)
⊖ Acton Town

Bounded to the east by the North Circular and to the south by the M4 and the Martini Tower, Gunnersbury Park is a 185-acre open green space on the borders of Ealing and Acton. An estate since the Middle Ages, it is now dominated by the two stucco halls—Gunnersbury Park and Gunnersbury House—which, last owned by the Rothschilds, now form a museum devoted to the heritage of Ealing and Hounslow. But it's the grounds that make it extraordinary: a surprising secret garden in one of those parts of London dominated by the incessant buzz of modern transportation systems—the roads, the tube, the permanent throttle back of jets on their Heathrow landing pattern.

The best way to experience Gunnersbury is to turn immediately to the right once you get through the front gates: through a small garden protected from the road by a high brick wall, past the Temple and the boating pond—which in summer is full of delighted childish squeals—and westwards to the large open space which rises northwards from the lights of the M4—partially obscured by huge poplars—to the detached thirties houses that front on Popes Lane. In the far southwest corner, there is the Folly and the Potomac Lake: a small pond constructed out of a clay pit that plays host to meditative night-time fisherman.

Space in London is highly concentrated, and one of the things that has always amazed me about Gunnersbury Park is that you can be so close to major roads and yet still feel so secluded. The walk along the south side is completely covered by an umbrella of horse chestnuts—a deep boskiness that protects you until you walk back up north for the first proper view of the great house that you approach up a sharp incline to the long terrace. Walking to the west, you get a full view of the Orangery before returning, via the cafe, to the Temple and the exit—a 45-minute or so pause from the stomach churning exigencies of metropolitan life.

Before my parents moved to W8 in 1967, Gunnersbury was my local park: we lived a quarter of a mile away in Baronsmede, while my grandparents built their detached thirties property, Manor House, right opposite Gunnersbury's front gates. This suburban corner is central to who I am and now that I no longer live in London, I revisit it as a touchstone, of the way things were, are and still might be. My favourite time is at dusk, when there's no one around except the owls and, in summer, the bats: the familiar views (which to some might seem banal) remind me of my good fortune in having this free, imaginative space on my childhood doorstep.

JON SAVAGE
Historian of popular culture

Bedford Park

1875, Norman Shaw
Bedford Park W4 (Not on map)
⊖ Turnham Green

Bedford Park, begun in 1875, was the first planned garden suburb. Its significance was first noted by Herman Muthesius in his book *Das Englische Haus*. John Betjeman suggested it was England's greatest contribution to international architecture. Designed largely by Norman Shaw, it also has buildings by E. W. Godwin, E. J. May and Maurice Adams.

PETER MURRAY
Architectural impresario

HAMPSTEAD & THE NORTH

HAMPSTEAD & THE NORTH

1 Freud Museum
2 St. John's Church
3 Former home of Lord Alfred Douglas
4 St. John Graveyard
5 Former residence of General Charles de Gaulle
6 Abernethy House
7 Fenton House
8 Sun House

9 Louis Patisserie
10 Holly Bush Pub
11 Keats's House
12 House designed by Erno Goldfinger
13 Livingstone Studio (see p. 110)
14 Parliament Hill Café
15 Highgate Ponds
16 Kenwood House
17 Highgate Cemetery
18 Hill Garden
19 Golders Hill Park

HAMPSTEAD & THE NORTH

11.1 Freud Museum

20 Maresfield Gardens NW3, ☎ 020 7435 2002
or 020 7435 5267
⊖ Finchley Road

In a perilous last-ditch flight from the Nazis, Sigmund Freud arrived in London with his family in 1938, moving into the substantial red brick house in Hampstead which he predicted would be "his last address on this planet." The following year he died of cancer of the throat. This, the most atmospheric of all London museums, is strangely little known. At its heart is Freud's own study and consulting room, drawing its peculiar aura of enchantment from his famous collection of antiquities in bronze, stone, terra cotta, sent on from Vienna, and enriched by the colour and texture of the carpets and hangings. Most magnificent of these is the five-sided deep red and blue rug woven by one of the tribes of the Qashaqua'i Confederacy of Western Iran draped over the couch employed by Freud for his analyses. Dream on.

FIONA MACCARTHY
Biographer and critic

RECOMMENDED READING
Freud Museum, *20 Maresfield Gardens: A guide to the Freud Museum*, Serpent's Tail, 1998.

11.2 St. John's Church

1745–1747, John Sanderson, with many additions later on
Church Row NW3, ☎ 020 7794 5808
⊖ Hampstead

Hampstead's parish register, which was started in 1560, contains the entry "Noe burialls in 1566." The present parish church, St. John's, wasn't built until 1747, which means the graveyard is a better place for making contact with earlier centuries. The first parish church, St Mary's, existed in the 13th century and in 1837, when Constable was buried at the bottom of the slope, there were several layers of older bones beneath his coffin.

Inside the wrought iron gates, you have to duck under an overgrown holly bush and make your way down an uneven path between tombstones that have been tilted by subsidence to eccentric angles, while many have been damaged by the ice of successive winters.

Only a minority of the inscriptions is still legible. Erosion, moss, ice and stains on the stone have damned some of the dead to anonymity, while other headstones have been overpowered by shrubs, ivy, weeds, brambles and pine needles aspiring to the condition of compost. Some tombstones, once proudly vertical, are horizontal and fragmented, while others, flat and horizontal from the outset, are modestly pursuing the coffins into the earth.

Once I was told off here by a man in a raincoat. Why was I letting my daughter dance on his grandfather's grave? What were my religious beliefs? But, far from being vertically in line with the stone, the old man's remains would have been shifted by subterranean movements. Other bones were below the small feet.

RONALD HAYMAN
Writer

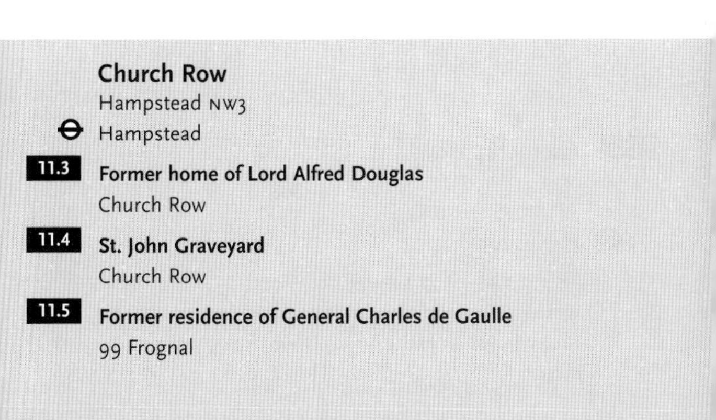

Church Row
Hampstead NW3
⊖ Hampstead

11.3 **Former home of Lord Alfred Douglas**
Church Row

11.4 **St. John Graveyard**
Church Row

11.5 **Former residence of General Charles de Gaulle**
99 Frognal

1.25 **French House**

49 Dean Street W1

The best walk in London is down Church Row in NW3. After his exile and disgrace as the boyfriend of Oscar Wilde, Lord Alfred Douglas lived here, though I don't know at which number. You could ring all the bells and ask. At the end of the road there is a ravishing little graveyard to the right which contains the remains of Hugh Gaitskell, Kay Kendall, Anton Walbrook (the ringmaster from *La Ronde*) and Joan Collins's mother. Our Lady guards Beerbohm Tree. To the left, in the grounds of the church itself, you will find the grave of John Harrison—immortalised by Michael Gambon in the television film of *Longitude*. You will also get an extraordinary view south towards the river. Then you should head on to Frognal, turn right, and at number 99 you will find the house where General de Gaulle lived as leader of the Free French throughout the Second World War. I find it heartstopping to think of him here, directing the French war effort from a house in Hampstead. Of course if you want to follow the theme of the Resistance, you then have to go to the French House in Soho to see where de Gaulle's juniors all ate and drank. But, for me, the pub will never be as evocative as the big, leafy house in North London.

DAVID HARE
Playwright

11.6 **Abernethy House**

1819

7 Heath Street NW3

Hampstead

"Robert Louis Stevenson slept here . . . " is among the world's most common graffiti. Recently, I discovered a very pretty house in Hampstead, where he stayed for about a month in 1874: Abernethy House, in Mount Vernon. No cars and few pedestrians pass by. From the window giving on to Holly Place, Stevenson spied some little girls playing with skipping ropes, which moved him to write the essay "Notes on the Movements of Young Children."

JAMES CAMPBELL
Writer and editor

11.7 Fenton House

1693
Hampstead Grove NW3, ☎ 020 7435 3471
Closed from November through mid-March
⊖ Hampstead

Fenton House has a secret garden, high-walled in warm, worn red brick, where roses and clematis climb, and flowering terraces lead to a quiet, ancient, gnarled orchard. The house, a perfect example of London Queen Anne, as copied in Victorian doll's houses, stands back from the street on Windmill Hill, Hampstead. The museum shows musical instruments—especially 17th- and 18th-century harpischords—and in the summer there are concerts. It's such a hidden place of enchantment, I'm loath to give away its presence.

MARINA WARNER
Writer

Highgate and Hampstead Architecture Stroll

⊖ Highgate

Highpoint I and II
Highgate North Hill N6 (see p. 196) (Not on map)

Studio House
1939, Tayler & Green
Duke's Head Yard N6 (Not on map)

11.17 Highgate Cemetery
Swains Lane N6

11.12 House designed by Ernö Goldfinger
2 Willow Road NW3

11.8 **Sun House**
1934-1935, Maxwell Fry
Frognal Way NW3

11.9 **Louis Patisserie**
32 Heath Street NW3, 020 7435 9908

11.10 **Holly Bush Pub**
22 Holly Mount NW3, 020 7435 2892

English insularity kept Modern architecture at bay in the early 20th century, and only in the 1930s was there a scattered, rather timorous acceptance of it. There is no better way to see this belated embrace of Modernism than to spend an afternoon walking between Highgate and Hampstead. Take the underground to Highgate and head for North Hill where you will find two blocks of flats by the Russian *émigré* Berthold Lubetkin: Highpoint I (1933–1935) and Highpoint II (1938). Both are indebted to Le Corbusier but the latter upset the purists with two Erechtheum caryatids at its entrance—a definite hint of the surreal.

Continue into Highgate village and, off High Street, enter inconspicuous Duke's Head Yard for Tayler & Green's 1939 Studio House, with more Corbusian echoes. Cemetery-lovers might then detour down Swain's Lane to visit London's most atmospheric example. Otherwise take the narrow, continually interesting Fitzroy Park to the edge of Hampstead Heath. Choose from a variety of routes and enjoy expansive views towards the city as you make for 2 Willow Road on the far side of the Heath. This was designed by the Hungarian *émigré* Ernö Goldfinger and, owned by the National Trust, is now open to the public. A walk up Willow Road brings you to Hampstead and your final destination—Maxwell Fry's white-walled Sun House of 1934–1935, in Frognal Way, which, well-maintained, still radiates the excitement of the new. There's an excellent patisserie in nearby Heath Street (opposite the end of 18th century Church Row); or have a beer in the Holly Bush.

ANDREW MEAD
Architectural writer

11.11 Keats's House

Wentworth Place, Keats Grove NW3, ☎ 020 7435 2062
Hampstead

He was only 25 when he died, but by then he'd written some of the greatest poems in the English language. Tuberculosis overtook him before he could marry the girl he loved, but they had one summer of intense happiness, living in semi-detached houses with a shared garden and a thin party wall.

At the end of 1818, the 23-year-old John Keats moved from lodgings in Well Walk, Hampstead, to share a nearby house with a friend, Charles Brown. Keats paid him £5 a month for the room and the meals. The bigger house on the other side of the thin wall belonged to a friend of theirs, Charles Wentworth Dilke. Then only two years old, the houses were jointly known as Wentworth Place, and they'd been designed to look like a single house. One front door was in the middle, with the other tucked inconspicuously around the corner of the building.

Nobody now thinks of Hampstead as being outside London, but two years later, when the painter Constable settled his ailing wife and their children into Well Walk, he wrote: "I'm glad to get them out of London for every reason." Hampstead was still a secluded village, surrounded by fields. There were encampments of gypsies on the Heath, and cattle grazed there.

The eighteen-year-old Fanny Brawne was living with her widowed mother, a younger brother, and a younger sister in a cottage at the corner of Downshire Hill and the road which was called Red Lion Hill until it became Keats Grove. After meeting Fanny at the end of 1818, he described her as "beautiful and elegant, graceful, silly, fashionable and strange." A few days later he wrote: "she is ignorant—monstrous in her behaviour—flying out in all directions." But soon they were unofficially engaged.

In the spring of 1819, when Dilke moved out of his

house, the Brawnes moved in. Keats and Fanny saw each other almost every day, and went for walks on the Heath. She inspired some of his best poems, and by May he'd completed five odes, including the one to the nightingale, which took him only a few hours. He wrote it under a plum tree in the garden.

Brown always let his house in the summer, and Keats, who went with him to the Isle of Wight and Winchester, suffered such pangs of jealousy that he wanted to break off the engagement. He told Fanny he was trying "to force you from my mind . . . I love you too much to venture to Hampstead. I feel it is not paying a visit but venturing into a fire." He decided to live in Westminster and work as a journalist. But seeing her when he went to collect his things from the house, he had to give up the idea of leaving her. "You dazzled me. There's nothing in the world so bright and delicate."

Told by his doctors to spend the next winter in Italy, Keats left Wentworth Place in September. Fanny prepared his clothes for the journey, and lined his travelling cap with silk. His last words to her were written from Naples in a letter to her mother dated 24 October 1820, but he'd written his last full letter to Fanny in August. "I wish I was either in your arms full of faith or that a Thunder bolt would strike me."

Unlike the lovers, the semi-detached houses were soon married. They were bought at the end of the 1830s by a retired actress, Eliza Chester, who'd been known as "Prinny's Last Fling," Prinny being the Prince Regent. Making the two houses into one, she had the staircase removed from the smaller house, and in the bigger she made the two parlours into one, adding a wing to contain another large drawing-room. But you can still see most of the original furniture, and three locks of Keats's brown hair.

RONALD HAYMAN
Writer

11.14 **Parliament Hill Cafe**
Parliament Hill Fields, Highgate Road NW3,
tel. 020 7485 6606

Don't miss the cafe at the bottom of Parliament Hill Fields. Go on a winter morning and you'll have it all to yourself. You can get an okay cappuccino and leaf through back copies of *Ham and High*. Then walk along, past the Lido and the strength-through-joy running track, and all of London is spread out on your left. If it's clear you'll see from Canary Wharf right across to Hammersmith. The London Eye presents a graceful ellipse bang in the middle of the frame, just between the Post Office Tower and Big Ben, and if it's really clear you'll see the south downs, and get a sense of the scale of the city sprawl, and its green boundaries. Walk past the empty benches with their maudlin dedications where dozens of over-fed crows congregate listlessly in the cold weather. Then turn right up the hill, past grand Hampstead houses. Twenty minutes' brisk walk will bring you to Kenwood House (see p. 193).

ROGER MICHELL
Director

Hampstead Stroll
Hampstead

11.15 **Highgate Ponds**
Hampstead Heath, east side NW3

11.16 **Kenwood House**
Hampstead Lane NW3, 020 8348 1286

11.7 **Fenton House**
Hampstead Grove NW3, 020 7435 3471

11.10 **Holly Bush Pub**
22 Holly Mount NW3, 020 7435 2892

A perfect summer's day: a swim in one of the ponds on Hampstead Heath, then a stroll to Kenwood House to look at Rembrandt's self-portrait, then a walk into Hampstead via the row of cottages in Mansfield Place and a wander around the garden of Fenton House, ending with a drink at the Holly Bush Pub.

DEBORAH MOGGACH
Writer

11.15 Summer Swims at Highgate Ponds

Hampstead Heath, east side NW3
Open from May to September. Take the tube to Kentish Town, to catch the #214 bus up Highgate Road. Get off at Parliament Hill and walk up the hill. Turn left onto Millfield Lane, which leads you into the ponds. This should take about a half-hour. You can also take the overland rail (Broad Street Line) to Gospel Oak station, which is just by Parliament Hill. Continue as above. For more information, phone the London Borough of Camden Parks Department, at 020 7974 1693.
Kentish Town; rail: Gospel Oak

A personal favourite with visitors in the summer are the ponds at Highgate. It surprises out-of-towners who have suffered a hot day of London tubes and stress that you can swim in fresh water in the open air—with a view over the City. There are separate men's and women's ponds (the water flows through the women's first!) and in late summer, the temperature is delightful. There are no lockers, the atmosphere is very relaxed; it is not at all "naturist;" indeed, the mix is indicative of London's cultural diversity: Orthodox Jews with their ringlets pinned up; old, young, fit and unfit. The women's pond, I'm told, is rather more sociable.

I recommend the stiff walk back up the hill to The Flask Tavern (77 West Highgate Hill N6, 020 8340 7260), a Georgian pub at Highgate Village; if it is getting cold by then, they have braziers outside.

IAN KELLY
Actor and writer

11.16 Kenwood House

Hampstead Lane NW3, 020 8348 1286

Highate, Archway

Go to Kenwood for one of the great picture collections in the capital (free). Then make for the Heath, just beyond the Kenwood fence, where there are fantastic trees for the small and the agile to climb and places to picnic where you won't be disturbed all afternoon.

GILLIAN DARLEY
Architectural writer

The best way to explore the grounds is on a twenty-minute circular lakeside walk. Go through the trellis tunnel at the side of the house, cross the terrace, take the steps down the grassy bank and cross the fenced pasture to the right of the lake, looking back at the house to take in the fall of light on its façade. Cross the bridge to the right of the lake, follow the path through the woods, bearing left, and you'll end up back at the Brew House Cafe, situated behind the house in the old stable block. Inside can be quite crowded, but there is a spacious and sheltered walled garden.

Locals visit Kenwood all year round to walk, to jog and to picnic, but seasonal highlights include the banks of daffodils in early spring, the massive flowering rhododendrons in May and the lakeside classical concerts programmed for many evenings throughout the summer. One tip: if you drive to Kenwood, avoid the cramped car park. Leave your car on Hampstead Lane, just opposite Compton Avenue, and enter by the East Lodge. The secluded right-hand path takes you in style right to the front door.

CHRISTOPHER GEELAN AND SARAH GORDON
Theatre producers

Self-Portrait

About 1630, Rembrandt

The Rembrandt self portrait, tucked away in the leafy setting of Kenwood House on Hampstead Heath, has haunted me since I was a teenager, a hundred years ago. Yes, there is a sunny Franz Hals there and yes, there is an exquisite Vermeer there. But the Rembrandt just hypnotises me, as it always has. The eyes of the master are tragic and yet the face and the whole pose are full of dignity and inner strength. I never can take my eyes off the picture and if my eyes can stray for a short while onto the marvellously sumptuous painting of the fur on his garment, they soon lock back onto his eyes, sad and defiant. Possibly the greatest painter who ever lived and certainly one of his greatest paintings. And so close to my doorstep when I grew up in Hampstead. I was lucky. It was just luck the painting was there and I was so nearby. And it will always be there!

BERNARD JACOBSON
Art gallery director

Coach House / Brew House Cafe

020 8341 5384

On a sunny morning in spring or summer or crisp days in autumn, go and eat breakfast in the Coach House at Kenwood. Load your tray with eggs, bacon, sausage, grilled tomato, mahogany-brown tea and carry it out to one of the tables in the garden. You can look at the fig trees and argue about whether a fig has ever ripened in England, you can fend off the sparrows and robins, and when you have finished your breakfast you can stroll round the corner for a look at the best small art collection in the world.

NICCI GERRARD AND SEAN FRENCH
Novelists and journalists

11.17 Highgate Cemetery

Swains Lane N6, 020 8340 1834

The cemetery is divided into East and West sections. The East, home to Karl Marx's grave, is open from 10am until 4pm every day. Visiting the West requires a guided tour, offered 12noon, 2pm and 4pm on weekdays and from 11am, hourly until closing, on weekends, for a small entry fee.

 Highgate, Archway

When I was working as a writer in Hampstead I needed somewhere peaceful but stimulating to walk to in the afternoons. It was a long journey across the Heath to Highgate Cemetery, but when one got there one entered a mysterious world like a walled-in but nevertheless apparently boundless jungle—thick undergrowth and huge trees encroaching on elaborate tombs like the half-hidden temples of Cambodia. There were domes, porticos, spires; a sunken mausoleum like an ancient Egyptian excavation; a colossal monument to a horse. At the centre, like the presiding deity of a sacred grove, there was on its plinth the massive bust of Karl Marx, his formidable head jammed down onto his shoulders, in an area kept reverentially clear around him with perhaps a faded wreath or two. There was a strange potency in the great apostle of materialism being commemorated in such a wild and almost mystical place. The Cemetery had long since been closed to new burials, and in the 1970s it was only open to the public on certain days of the week or year—so this added to the sense of secrecy and taboo.

NICHOLAS MOSLEY
Novelist

11.18 Hill Garden

Inverforth Close NW3

Hampstead

If you like surprises, this is a must—London's most secret garden. Secluded and beautiful, this is quintessential landscape architecture. The rolling hillside is defined by the colonnaded walkway, with its painted Tuscan Doric columns, quasi-temples and pagodas, its rhythm reflected in its stone paving. Formal lawns and pools have been inserted into the hillside, and wonderful trees and borders are all around. It is all immaculately kept, the colonnade has been recently restored, and on most days you have this haven of peaceful contemplation all to yourself.

EDWARD BURD
Architect

11.19 Golders Hill Park

Hampstead NW3

Golders Green, Hampstead

Less well-known than the main Hampstead Heath, a visit to Golders Hill Park (at the far west corner of the Heath) is a perfect afternoon out. The formal Flower Garden and Pergola provide respite from the centre of London, while the new play structures entertain young children for hours. Inflatables and a variety of clowns and magicians visit Golders Hill Park in the summer holidays and the Italian ice cream parlour has some of the best homemade ice cream in London.

FELICITY LUNN
Curator and lecturer

Highpoint I & II

1933–1935 (I) and 1938 (II), Berthold Lubetkin (Tecton)

Highgate North Hill N6 (Not on map)

Highgate

Conventional plans are transformed by simple modernist devices. The caryatids on II are either announcing the decline of modernism or indicating Lubetkin's breadth of sources.
ROBERT LIVESEY
Architect

Queen's Wood

Highgate N6 (Not on map)
Highgate

A true gem of untouched woodland next to Highgate Tube station. No views, no children's playgrounds, no picnickers, just a valley of ancient trees with an empty, rundown pond in the middle. The wood is perfect for that half-hour of silent commune with the wood sprites, an antidote to the peopled greenery that makes up most other London parks.

Each tree and overgrown pathway stands in silent tribute to one of those grand preservation campaigns that explode magnificently into the public consciousness and then disappear into the mists. In the 1890s, the battle for Churchyard Bottom, as the wood was less elegantly known, occupied the columns of local and national newspapers as well as a good chunk of parliamentary time. An Appeal Committee included such forgotten heroes as The Rt. Hon. G. J. Shaw-Lefevre and Thomas Skinner Esq. (What fun to be able to rescue, even momentarily, two of their names.) It was set up to pay off the rapacious Ecclesiastical Commissioners who considered that making money for the propagation of religion served a higher purpose than preserving the environment. The huge sum of £30,000 was eventually raised to protect the trees from the urban spread that ate up the countryside of North London in the 20th century.

A hundred years ago the renamed Queen's Wood was well looked after, boasting a fence, a lodge and a tearoom as well as four full-time keepers. The woods were in constant use as a place of escape for the masses on their way to Alexandra Palace, that Victorian folly, first broadcast home to the BBC and now an ice-rink with a view. Today a penurious local council leaves the place to run wild. Nature flourishes gloriously in this lack of attention—an oasis for foxes, birds and the occasional strange human souls doing their own things. The tearoom, recently reopened just off Muswell Hill Road, serves a delicious and suitably organic mix of hot food and cakes.

So if you are ever wavering over a contribution to a campaign to save something for posterity and think "what's the point," catch the Northern Line to Highgate and meditate under one of the great beeches in Queen's Wood.

ANGUS MACQUEEN
Documentary film-maker

Alexandra Palace

Originally completed in 1873 by Alfred Meeson and John Johnson; rebuilt in 1875 by Johnson.

Alexandra Palace Way, Wood Green N22, 020 8365 2121
(Not on map)
railway: Alexandra Palace, from King's Cross

Every world city has its white elephants; what would we do without them? London has a fine example on its northern rim: Ally Pally, opened in May 1873 and destroyed by fire within two weeks. Rebuilt in two years it has had a chequered history and was the site of the BBC's first public television broadcast. I like it most on the closest Saturday night to the 5th of November when the skies light up with the Ally Pally fireworks, commemorating itself as much as Guy Fawkes, and all across the city bonfires burn.

ROMESH GUNESEKERA
Author

Dawn Chorus and Bat Walks

Both walks run during the summer months, peaking in July and August.

Hampstead Heath NW3

Dates and times of the Hampstead Heath walks are available from the Information Centre, Parliament Hill Lido, ☎ 020 7485 3873.

⊖ Hampstead, Belsize Park

Waterlow Park

Waterlow Park walks are announced on their notice board. For updated information, call the London Wildlife Trust: ☎ 020 7261 0447 or check their website at www.wildlifetrust.org.uk; or the Bat Conservation Group: ☎ 020 7627 2629, or check www.bats.org.uk.

⊖ Archway

If you can get to Hampstead Heath by 4am on an April or May morning you can set off in the company of other people you can't yet see and be led into the woods. At first there's nothing to hear, then a few peep peeps, then all within a few minutes a good racket sets up as you greyly begin to make out your companions. When I've been, the guide's style has been an appealing mixture of the laid-back and the knowledgeable: able to chat, smoke and yet simultaneously single out all sorts of different bird voices. Some are familiar enough, even in London, but others, like those of migrants, Black Cap and Chiffchaff, can only be heard for those few weeks of spring.

The bat walks start on summer evenings and attract all sorts of people, some keenly carrying little black electronic boxes called Bat Detectors. Even if the bats don't show up it's a lovely walk. But they generally do, and then the Bat Detector owners get very excited, sorting out which bat is which according to the frequency of its squeaks. What I like are the names of the bats: Pipistrelle, Daubenton's, Noctule, Natterer (this last, being rarer here, the cause of great jubilation when it appears).

There are also bat walks in Waterlow Park, Highgate, from which you get a wonderful view of London—so good that Sir Sydney Waterlow, Lord Mayor of London, 1872–1873, donor of the park, has been standing on his plinth, pipe in one hand, hat and umbrella in the other, admiring it ever since he was placed there, almost a century ago.

RUTH PAVEY

Reviewer, journalist, and teacher

THE EAST END & BEYOND

THE EAST END & BEYOND

1 Christ Church, Spitalfields
2 Spitalfields Market
3 A. Gold
4 "I've Seen the Future"
5 Brick Lane Beigel Bake
6 Boundary Estate
7 Columbia Road Flower Market
8 White Cube 2

9 Geffrye Museum
10 Bethnal Green Museum of Childhood
11 York Hall Baths (see p. 168)
12 The Green Bridge, Mile End Park
13 Trinity Green
14 Wilton's Music Hall
15 Jack the Ripper Walking Tour

THE EAST END & BEYOND

12.1 Christ Church, Spitalfields

1714–1729, Nicholas Hawksmoor

Commercial Street, Spitalfields E1, ☎ 020 7247 7202

⊖ Aldgate East, Liverpool Street

When I first discovered this astonishing Baroque *tour de force*—by an architect whose name was almost forgotten—it was full of dust and broken pews, with water dripping though the ceiling and pigeons nesting in the nave. The churchyard was full of meths drinkers and was known locally as Itchy Park. Miraculously, though, Christ Church escaped collapse or demolition. Slowly it is being restored to its bright, white pristine beauty. You can hear music within it sometimes. And it stands, like an angular, awkward, strange bird, in one of the oldest districts of London, with the City to one side and the heartland of London's Bangladeshi community behind. See it, and be amazed, and go on to discover Hawksmoor's other masterpieces, two more of them also in the East End: St. Anne's, Limehouse (see p. 219) and St. George's in the East (Cannon Street Road E1).

PAUL BARKER
Writer and broadcaster

RECOMMENDED READING
Kerry Downes, *Hawksmoor*, Thames and Hudson, 1969.

Classic "piling it on." Start with a funky temple. Add a triumphal arch, a few volutes, a base, smaller base, and end the magic trick with a hanging handkerchief. Inside, the church has a Gothically proportioned space made with classical elements.

ROBERT LIVESEY
Architect

12.2 Spitalfields Market

Commerical Street E1, ☎ 020 7377 1496
Between Lamb and Brushfield Streets
⊖ Liverpool Street

Not far from the commercial heart of London, the City, lies Spitalfields. This area was once a rich suburb populated by wealthy weavers and cloth merchants, many of whom translated their earnings into large and fashionable houses. Today it preserves, better than any other part of London, a feel for the 18th century. Go to Liverpool Street tube and cross Bishopsgate into Spitalfields Market. On the far side is Christ Church, the parish church. From here abandon yourself to the maze of ancient terraces and afterwards choose a pub or bar in the market and relax.

SIMON THURLEY
Director, Museum of London

Spitalfields Stroll

⊖ Aldgate East, Liverpool Street

A wonderful dusk walk: 18th-century Spitalfields streets—Princelet, Folgate Street, gazing into beautiful panelled rooms, and ending with an Indian meal in Brick Lane.

DEBORAH MOGGACH
Writer

12.3 A. Gold

42 Brushfield Street E1, ☎ 020 7247 2487
⊖ Liverpool Street

My current favourite weekend activity is bicycling to A. Gold, a small specialist grocer and wine merchant alongside Spitalfields Market, close to the City and Liverpool Street station. My route takes me through Brick Lane and the small side streets of this part of 18th-century London, now smartened up as if it were a piece of New England.

CHARLES SAUMAREZ SMITH
Director, National Portrait Gallery

12.4 "I've Seen the Future"

Docklands Light Railway (DLR) to West India Quay, then onwards to Canary Wharf
railway: DLR from Bank tube station

Possibly one of the most romantic evenings to be had in London begins by taking the Docklands Light Railway from Bank station. After the initial sci-fi departure into the open air, the bizarre mix of old, new and barren that is Docklands opens up before you. Ideally take the line as far as West India Quay and cross the Future Systems Bridge over to Canary Wharf. Canary Wharf by night almost lends plausibility to conspiracy theorists who suggest it is a beacon to aliens, falling as it does on several significant ley lines.

SHEZ 360
Artist

12.5 Brick Lane Beigel Bake

159 Brick Lane E1, 020 7729 0616
Shoreditch, Aldgate East

Publishing the secret haunts of your home town seems an exercise in reckless bragging, trading the kudos of showing off your insider knowledge for the loss of your favourite cafe or quiet retreat. But the Brick Lane Beigel Bake, well. . . it's one of those city institutions that can barely be described as a secret anymore, yet for any visitor it still gives off that strange sense of satisfaction at having found a gem away from the beaten track. Open 24/7. Smoked salmon and cream cheese bagel only 95p. Say no more.

DAN FOX
Writer and editor

12.6 Boundary Estate

1899, London County Council

The Boundary Estate E2 is approximately bordered by Virginia Road at its north end, Swanfield Street at its east end, Old

Nichol Street at its south end, Boundary Street at its west end, with Arnold Circus in the center.

 Shoreditch

Southeast of Shoreditch Church lies the Boundary Estate, a whole area of beautiful red brick Arts and Crafts tenement buildings that were built to replace the infamous Jago, the Victorian Hell's Kitchen of London. Streets lined with plane trees radiate out from Arnold Circus. The bandstand in the centre of the Circus sits on a mound made from the rubble of the 19th-century slums. Visit on a Sunday morning when a two-minute walk north takes you to Columbia Road Flower Market (cappuccinos and exotic plants), or a two-minute walk south takes you to Brick Lane Market (stolen bikes and three-card tricks).

CORNELIA PARKER
Artist

12.7 Columbia Road Flower Market

Columbia Road E5
Open Sunday mornings.

Bethnal Green

My favourite place is ephemeral. It comes into being on Sunday mornings, at the moment the trucks wake me up delivering their goods. It begins to disintegrate after 2:30pm when what produce remains is trundled back into vans by people shouting in cockney accents, or is bought cheaply, surreptitiously and illegally, by locals like me. I speak of that oldest and most famous flower market—Columbia Road. Every Sunday morning my studio (thirty seconds' walk from the florabundal epicentre), is garlanded with kangaroo paw, lilies, parrot tulips, tuberose—proof that nature still exists somewhere, even during a London winter.

The market provides many subsidiary attractions. For example, when the English buy bedding plants, they cheer up, and sometimes smile at complete strangers. Of course, every kind of human creature (and dog) can be studied in the market, not just the natives. Lately the Brit Art Move-the market, not just the natives. Lately the Brit Art Movement has turned this once flea-bitten area into the most fashionable address in the city. Where once there were workmen's cafes and cabinet makers along Columbia Road, there are now antique shops and bijou bagel vendors. A classical music quartet has started busking on the corner and a red van sells the best coffee east of the London wall. The little fish-shop with the striped awning is still there though, selling whelks and eels.

Once, on a Sunday morning, I was practising my piano with the French doors open. A flower-buying crowd gathered on the street below and started clapping. The delight of Sunday mornings compensates for East End Sunday afternoons.

ROBYN DAVIDSON
Travel writer

12.8 **White Cube 2**
2000, Rundell Associates
48 Hoxton Square N1, ☎ 020 7930 5373
⊖ Old Street, exit 2

The former site of my publishers, Duckworths, 48 Hoxton Square, was bought by dealer to the Sensation era, Jay Jopling, and converted into a conceptual art nexus for this, London's version of New York's Soho. A luminous white cube, indeed, filled with works, depending on Jopling's latest discovery, from Gilbert and George to Damien Hirst to Sarah Morris. Take a walk outside and the full force of an area described by the *Evening Standard* as the art/fashion centre of the universe will appear to be entirely underwhelming. But then you notice the galleries and bars opening up almost before your eyes, and having got your eye in, there'll be no looking back. Soon you'll be wanting one of those half-million pound loft conversions, and wondering how you ever lived without Tracey Emin. She often thinks the same thing.

PHILIP HOARE
Writer, curator and presenter

RECOMMENDED READING

Johnnie Shand Kydd, *Spit Fire*, Violette Editions, 1997 (UK); Distributed Art Publications, 1997 (US).

Dazed and Confused Magazine

The Number 11

Bus route beginning at Liverpool Street Station E1.

Liverpool Street

I love travelling upstairs on the front seat of London's double decker buses to get a bird's eye view of London. My favourite bus journey is the number 11 route. Take it from the back of Liverpool Street Station. It travels down Threadneedle Street (Bank of England) through the City, past St. Paul's Cathedral, down Fleet Street (one of the most wonderful streets in London) past the law courts to the Aldwych on to the Strand. Past Charing Cross, Nelson's column, down Whitehall (10 Downing Street) past the Houses of Parliament and on to Victoria. Then you get to Sloane Square and King's Road (full of great clothes shops). Get off at World's End and walk back down King's Road towards Sloane Square and shop till you drop, ending up at Peter Jones (Sloane Square, 020 7730 3434), my favourite department store.

CORNELIA PARKER

Artist

12.9 Geffrye Museum

Old wing: 1714, unknown architect but funded by the Ironmonger's Company; new wing completed 1998, Branson Coates Architecture.

136 Kingsland Road E2, 020 7739 9893

From tube, take bus #243, Liverpool Street, then bus #242.

Old Street

I based the almshouse in my novel *Fish, Blood and Bone* on the austerely elegant 18th-century Geffrye Museum, where each room has been converted to show the art and interior design of different periods in British history—from darkly elaborate Elizabethan through the streamlined late 20th century of Tom Dixon leather chairs. My favourite local small museum, with an excellent free reading room and regular exhibitions, it's a must for every student or fan of design. There is a peaceful, period herb garden surrounding the building, a haven of green in the tarmac and tombstone grey of Kingsland Road, and a passable cafe in the Nigel Coates-designed wing (where the staircase resembles something from a Batman movie). For anything more than tea, though, it's better to sample one of the authentic Vietnamese eateries on South Kingsland Road, or walk a few blocks south, where Hoxton offers the latest in trendy London restaurants and bars.

LESLIE FORBES
Novelist

12.10 Bethnal Green Museum of Childhood

1860, J.W. Wild. Most of the building was originally part of the Victoria & Albert Museum, but was transported to this site and reconstructed by J.W.Wild in 1860.

Cambridge Heath Road and Old Ford Road E2,
020 8980 2415
Bethnal Green

For a touch of the country house in London, see the doll's houses or Baby Houses at the Bethnal Green Museum of Childhood, a branch of the Victoria & Albert Museum. The 18th-century Baby Houses were not on the whole made for children but for young women of aristocratic or gentle birth, as expensive miniatures in the spirit of a Cabinet of Curiosities: the best examples are works of art, possibly a little lost on children

JEREMY MUSSON
Editor

RECOMMENDED READING
Olivia Bristol and Leslie Geddes-Brown, *Doll's Houses*, Miller's Publications, 1997.
M. R. James, *The Haunted Doll's House*, 2nd edition, Penguin, 2000.
Halina Pasierbska, *Doll's House Furniture*, Shire Publications Ltd., 1998.

12.12 The Green Bridge, Mile End Park

2000, Piers Gough
Mile End Road E2
Mile End

This is a very "unambitious" idea which creates an ambitious result, unifying a park and regenerating an urban area. The delight in the "locals" is palpable, and hopefully it will have along term impact. And most of all it is joyous.
KAREN WRIGHT
Editor

12.13 Trinity Green

1695, possibly designed by Christopher Wren
Mile End Road E1
 Stepney, Mile End

I used to live in Trinity Green, Mile End Road. It is a collegiate style square with chapel and it was built—in cool, proportioned style—for mariners' widows whose husbands had not returned. So there are nautical references everywhere. Half of the Green was bombed in the Blitz, the other half is as it was—but you can't spot the joins. Trinity Green is a jewel, which until recently wasn't even mentioned in the *A-Z*. It was the subject of the very first volume of the *Survey of London*, written by the Arts and Crafts denizen C. R. Ashbee, who called it "an object lesson in national history." A neglected square of London.
CHRISTOPHER FRAYLING
Rector, Royal College of Art

RECOMMENDED READING

Alan Crawford, *C. R. Ashbee: Architect, Designer and Romantic Socialist*, Yale University Press, 1986.

12.14 Wilton's Music Hall

Opened in 1858 by John and Ellen Wilton. Closed in 1885 and opened as a church in 1888.

Grace Alley, off Cable Street, Whitechapel E1,

020 7702 9555

Tower Hill, Aldgate East

As the great actress Peggy Ashcroft once said, theatres either have an atmosphere or they don't. This one does, also a secrecy and a mystery, for no one knows about the place except a few film crews. Hidden away off Cable Street, Wilton's, London's first Victorian music hall, is a forgotten gem occasionally used for small-scale operas, commercial purposes, even private functions (the actor and writer Simon Callow threw a black and white fiftieth birthday party there). It reeks of the spirit of music hall, with its perfect rectangular proportions, barley sugar pillars and pretty balcony running right round the interior, which is narrow and high. Champagne Charlie sang his songs here in the 1860s, John Betjeman heroically saved the place from the bulldozers in the 1960s. And in the late 1990s, the Irish actress Fiona Shaw performed T. S. Eliot's poetic lamentation *The Waste Land*, the first live performance in more than a hundred years. The theatre came alive again in shudders and echoes of the past. But it does anyway, if you just poke your head through the door.

MICHAEL COVENEY

Critic

12.15 Jack the Ripper Walking Tour

For information, 020 7624 3978, or check local listings in "Around Town" section of *Time Out*.

Tower Hill

I know this sounds as corny as the wax works at Madame Tussauds, but trust me, it ain't. It's my favourite walk offered by The Original London Walks, the group that organizes hourly tours with subjects ranging from "Charles Dickens's London" to "Princess Diana's London," from "The Old Jewish Quarter Tour" to the "Beatles Magical Mystery." Show up at the tube stop, meet your guide, pay your £5 and you're off. In two hours, see and learn more about London than most Londoners will ever know in a lifetime. "Jack The Ripper Haunts" meets Sunday nights at 7:30PM at the Tower Hill tube and is led by Donald (the world's leading "Ripper-ologist") Rumbelow. He escorts his group through the East End of London, describing in gory detail the wheres and hows of each murder, finishing at The Ten Bells, the pub where the prostitute-victims drank their final gins. Despite initial protestations from visiting friends, they invariably return to my flat in a Victorian frenzy saying, "That was the best thing we've done in London."

GLEN ROVEN
Composer

Ridley Road Market

Dalston E8

From Liverpool Street, take bus #149; from Old Street, bus #243. (Not on map)

Liverpool Street, Old Street; railway: North London line to Dalston Central

If you savour the multicultural, head for Kingsland High Street in Dalston, Hackney. This bustling stretch of the Kingsland Road is crowded with nail parlours and barber shops, Turkish restaurants and pool halls, Irish pubs, cosmetic emporiums with a line in Voodoo, a Kentucky Fried Chicken and even a Percy Ingalls. New clubs open regularly, their façades as fortress-like as the infamous Four Aces around the corner in Dalston Lane.

Here among frail senior citizens, the aboriginal Hackneyites, are women swaddled in robes and veils and some of the best-dressed black youth in the metropolis. But the road's greatest attraction is its street market. Brick Lane is more fashionable, while Brixton's covered market is safer from the weather, but for economy and cheerful pandemonium, none compares with Ridley Road. It's served by flotillas of buses (numbers 76, 67, 243, 149), so leave the car on the fringes of Islington or take the North London line to Dalston Central just opposite the market entrance. Walking out of the station is like hurling yourself into a twenty-knot current of humanity. Best times to visit are Friday afternoons or Saturday mornings for the real bargains and the exotic fruit and vegetables. You'll find cheap clothing and CD's: Reggae, Turkish—traditional and pop—soul, salsa, Malian, and Golden Oldies. Enormous women's knickers flutter like acetate flags, a wonder to behold.

It wasn't always this way. During the 1940s when the area was a working class Jewish neighbourhood, the market was notorious as the scene of spectacular running battles between Oswald Mosley's fascists and the Communist Party along with Jewish commandoes from the 43 Group. Hundreds of local people attended political meetings, and police vans lined the surrounding streets waiting to collect those arrested. Mosley made his last public speech in nearby Hertford Road.

Today the shady aisles behind the barrows are permeated by the spicy-earthy smell of Africa, and Nigerian shops stock arcane vegetables, incense and the dried body parts of indeterminate species. Some of the merchandise is so mysterious it's difficult to tell whether it's animal, mineral, or vegetable, let alone what its function might be.

Be sure to go right to the market's end where you'll find the incomparable Turkish supermarket. Apart from the feta, olives and watermelon, there is a large bakery where your Turkish pizza is assembled while you watch, and gleaming glass cases display the freshest and most varied selection of *baklava* in London. Hot flat bread is stacked on high mobile wooden shelves from which you help yourself. Ridley Road raises the spirits and restores the soul. For more conventional urbanites or those who prefer to remain depressed, there's a Sainsbury's next door.
MARY FLANAGAN
Writer

RECOMMENDED READING
Morris Beakman, *The 43 Group*, Centreprise Publications, 1993 (US); 2000 (UK).
David Widgery, *Some Lives! A GP's East End*, Simon and Schuster, 1993.
Patrick Wright, *A Journey Through Ruins*, Paladin, 1992.
Iain Sinclair, *Lights Out for the Territory*, Granta, 1997.

Abney Park Cemetery

Opened 1840, buildings and landscapings by William Hosking
Stoke Newington Church Street N16, ☎ 020 7275 7557
(Not on map)
Bus: #73; railway: Stoke Newington

Abney Park is a romantic wilderness off Stoke Newington High Street and Church Street, every bit as interesting as Highgate Cemetery. There is a monument to Isaac Watts (hymn writer) who is actually buried in Bunhill Fields and General William Booth (founder of the Salvation Army) was buried here in 1912. But there are splendid urns, inscriptions, lions, angels, beasts, and a policeman's helmet, dogs and cruisers too. All part of life's rich pageant.
PIERS PLOWRIGHT
Radio producer

William Booth of the Salvation Army found his final resting place here. His tomb is quite a head-turner. And there are many others, equally appealing, some—my special favourites—with tiny, ancient photographic ceramics glued to the front of them (the dead staring blankly into the camera lens, and then beyond it, into eternity), others, with poignant poems—sometimes whole families, killed in influenza epidemics—many in terrible disrepair; fallen angels, lop-sided plinths, toppling urns.

Just outside, after your walk, you can order a pristine cappuccino at a tight-arsed but relentlessly bohemian local brasserie.

NICOLA BARKER
Novelist

Hackney Empire Theatre

1901, Frank Matcham
291 Mare Street E8, 020 8510 4500 (Not on map)
railway: Hackney Central

The greatest of the super-ornate Edwardian theatres. Thanks to an enlightened management it's still putting on real theatrical experiences, from opera to pantomime, not the made-for-radio stuff you get in the West End.

ROWAN MOORE
Architecture critic

The Narrow Way

Hackney E5
The northern end of Mare Street (Not on map)
railway: Hackney Central

On Saturday mornings in particular you get the great gamut of unofficial London glaring in your eyes and bawling in your ears. There's ancient history: a tower built by the Knights Templar lurks behind the HSBC Bank, last remnant of a church whose tree-lined yard still spreads out to the rear. It blooms with crocuses in February and offers many splendid drunks, some as aged and derelict as the lichen-spotted tombstones. The Narrow Way itself becomes a corridor of potential conversions. A full range of socialist revolutionaries vie for your attention, and you may also be wooed by environmentalists, pentecostalists and Rastafarians, though the occasional black Muslims will ignore you if your skin is white. There are Turkish fashions, Asian fashions, and a streetwise sporting goods store where I fit my kids with trainers and the staff have learned the hard way not to accept credit cards. There are thrift shops—"everything a pound"—exotic fancy goods shops, an outdoor flower stall, the world's funkiest McDonalds and, just around the bottom corner under the railway bridge, a cluster of nail parlours and a jeweller with a pawn department you could base a sitcom on. In all its hope and all its sorrow, the whole of inner city London life is here.

DAVE HILL
Journalist

The Mother's Square

1987–1990, HTA Architects Ltd, formerly Hunt Thompson Associates

Lower Clapton Road, Hackney E5
Behind Mother's Hospital (Not on map)
railway: Hackney Central, Clapton

Here, the powerful sense of place transcends the graffiti, derelict cars and rubbish, to prove that low cost architecture does not mean low quality—either of ambition, concept, design or construction. In an impoverished neighbourhood, this housing development, primarily for people on low incomes, shines like a jewel. The design is rigorous, with a nod toward Palladio, and flats, houses and old people's accommodation are all incorporated within it. If all social housing was like this, all social classes would be queuing up for the opportunity to live in it.

EDWARD BURD
Architect

Sutton House

1535

Homerton High Street E9, ☎ 020 8986 2264 (Not on map)
railway: Hackney Central

Extraordinary survival. Built for one of Henry VIII's strong-arm men, Sir Ralph Sadleir, who lived to sit in judgement on Mary, Queen of Scots, now National Trust. Exhibitions, concerts, excellent restaurant, rooms to hire. Splendid panelling—worth the effort to get there.

ANN SAUNDERS
Historian and editor

Victoria Park

Hackney E9 (Not on map)
railway: Cambridge Heath, Hackney Wick

Summer or winter, one of my favourite weekend haunts is Victoria Park—a sprawling green sanctuary dedicated to the people of the East End. A Victorian park through and through, it contains excavated lakes that serve as home to wayward boats and swans, a bowling green and a Chinese pagoda. A tea house turned cafe overlooks a large lake to the west and well-stocked pubs turn a healthy trade in fine food and drink at nearly every gate. In the eastern-most section, opposite the cricket pitches, are two recesses culled from the old London Bridge where one can sit and watch a long afternoon slowly pass. The area immediately surrounding the park retains a village-like feel and a number of galleries, cafes and delicatessens have slotted themselves in, adding organic fair and contemporary art to the local bagel or fish and chips. A haven for the urban rambler, Victoria Park can be reached from as far away as Little Venice in Maida Vale by walking or cycling along the tow path of the Grand Union and Regent's Canal. Dust off your CND (Campaign for Nuclear Disarmament) badge, bring along a book and settle in.

JOHN SLYCE
Writer and critic

Balfron Tower

1965, Ernö Goldfinger
St. Leonard's Road, Bow E14 (Not on map)
railway: Docklands Light Railway (DLR)

The figure of architect Ernö Goldfinger is by now more or less recognized—the house he built for himself at 2 Willow Road in Hampstead in 1938 is open to the public and his 31-storey residential block Trellick Tower of 1967 in the increasingly fashionable North Kensington is often seen in television programmes or in the background to commercials. But Balfron Tower, the slightly earlier and—at 27 storeys—smaller version in the unfashionable East End, is much less well-known. In combination, however, with Goldfinger's two later and lower blocks alongside, it forms a total composition that is arguably the most potent surviving example of his work and of Modern Movement urban design in London. This is brute concrete used like the noblest stone, but with a ferocity and spatial sophistication fully expressive of the turmoil of the 20th century. Though it is easier to reach since the development of the Docklands Light Railway, you will not be troubled by other tourists.

JAMES DUNNETT
Architect

RECOMMENDED READING

James Dunnett and Gavin Stamp, eds., with preface by Charlotte Perriand, *Ernö Goldfinger: Works 1*, Architectural Association, 1983.

Robert Elwall, *Ernö Goldfinger*, RIBA Drawings Monographs, no. 3, John Wiley and Son Ltd., 1996.

St. Anne's, Limehouse

Completed 1724, Nicholas Hawksmoor
Commerical Road E14, ☎ 020 7987 1502 (Not on map)
Services are held at 10:30am and 6pm, Sundays.
railway: Docklands Light Railway (DLR) to Westferry

I used to walk through the churchyard of St. Anne's, Limehouse every morning and evening and still regard St. Anne's

as Hawksmoor's least well-known and most architecturally satisfying church. It combines great simplicity in the view of the nave with his characteristic complexity in the composition of the entrance portico and tower. I miss it.
CHARLES SAUMAREZ SMITH
Director, National Portrait Gallery

RECOMMENDED READING
Peter Ackroyd, *Hawksmoor*, Penguin UK, 1993.

Back to front church. Entrance through the apse on the west side allows the sanctuary to have a wonderfully imposing façade on the east. The interior is the most Wren-like of Hawksmoor's churches. However, notice the scale of the "entablature" around the circular ceiling.
ROBERT LIVESEY
Architect

An East End Canal Walk

railway: Docklands Light Railway (DLR) to Limehouse

London's canals are an under-used and under-celebrated amenity. One of the most stimulating walks through the city's past can be found on the banks of the Grand Union Canal. Start early in the morning by taking the Docklands Light Railway to Limehouse and then follow the canal from the Limehouse Basin through the industrial wasteland of Mile End and the formal recreation ground of Victoria Park to the bustling streets of Islington, where a tunnel requires a short detour (and provides a convenient break for lunch). Rejoin the canal for a trip through the urban regeneration of King's Cross and the New Age attractions of Camden Lock before ending the afternoon in the more sedate settings of Regent's Park and Little Venice.
MICHAEL ARDITTI
Novelist

A Day in Epping Forest

Take the train from Liverpool Street station to Chingford and walk into Epping Forest. (Not on map)

⊖ Liverpool Street

Epping Forest, London's finest woodland, stretches north for almost six miles, a good day's outing, and absorbs thousands of recreationists into its glades of oak, beech, hornbeam and birch. Stop for tea amid throngs of bikers by the Robin Hood roundabout. Walk around two ancient hill forts, buried in woodland. Watch a cricket match on a clearing which is the lid of the sunken orbital M25 motorway. End the day by the log fire of the Forest Gate Inn (111 Bell Common, Epping, ☎01992 572 312), a down-to-earth hostelry, everything a country pub should be (and generally isn't).

MICHAEL HEBBERT
Professor of town planning

A Trip Downriver

Gallions Reach E16

From tube, change for the railway (North London line) to North Woolwich; or take the Docklands Light Railway (DLR) to Beckton

⊖ Stratford, Canning Town

When I first came to London I knew nobody and spent a month or two of Sundays walking about the place to fill in the time when I wasn't at work. My guide was a book—*Nairn's London* by the late Ian Nairn, who wrote about landscape and architecture with an eye for the unjustly neglected and the obscure, and daringly. Nairn was quite capable of estimating some suburban town hall as more glorious than the Taj Mahal, but his enthusiasm was infectious and he sent me (and many more) to places I would never otherwise have been.

Gallions Reach was one of them. This muddy stretch

of the lower Thames lies at the eastern end of the old Royal Docks. When I first went there, in 1970, yellow-funnelled freighters were unloading their cargoes in the Royal Albert and the pipes and retorts of the Beckton gasworks lay smoking and steaming over the way—close (it must be said) to the exit of the Northern Outfall Sewer. Freighters and gas works have gone long since (the ruins of the latter became a fake Vietnam for Kubrick's *Full Metal Jacket*), but the great architectural oddity of Gallions Reach remains as a listed building: the derelict Gallions Hotel (not open to public; Gallions Road, Royal Albert Dock E16). A piece of 1880s neo-Elizabethan, black and white with a red-tiled roof, it looks like a Surrey stockbroker's house which got built here through some ridiculous mistake. In fact, briefly and long ago, it served the travelling rich. Liners from the distant ports of the British Empire would stop at Gallions on their way to their final berth upriver, so that their passengers could disembark and reach the city more quickly. Boat trains met them. Embarking passengers waiting for outward-bound ships could eat, drink and rest at the Gallions Hotel. There's a line in Kipling: "Is it Tilbury and a tender, or Gallions and the Docks?"

The best way to get here is by train to North Woolwich or the Docklands Light Railway to Beckton, or by taking the ferry from Woolwich on the river's south bank. Go one way and come back another. North Woolwich has an interesting little railway museum and large sugar refinery on the river, where ships still call. Look west and you can see the Thames Barrier and planes taking off steeply from the City Airport. East lies the estuary and the sea. This is the very edge of London. If it's strangeness you're after, here it is. You might be inspired and think of the Thames as it appears in Kipling, Conrad and Dickens, the great imperial river—or you might agree with Captain Scott at the South Pole: "Dear God, this is an awful place."

Try to find a copy of Nairn's book (now out of print). Soon after I read it, I met the author and got to know him; we worked for the same newspaper for a while. A large man in a shabby blue suit with enormous appetites for Guinness and untipped Senior Service cigarettes; a person of sincere, powerful and eccentric enthusiasms. He would often answer the phone by barking "Woof, woof!" rather than the more normal "Hello." His books taught many of us to see London—and Britain—in more interesting ways.

IAN JACK
Editor

RECOMMENDED READING

Ian Nairn, *Nairn's London*, Penguin UK, 1966 (UK), o.p. Later reissued with a new commentary: *Nairn's London: The Classic Guidebook*, revisited by Peter Gasson, Penguin, 1988.

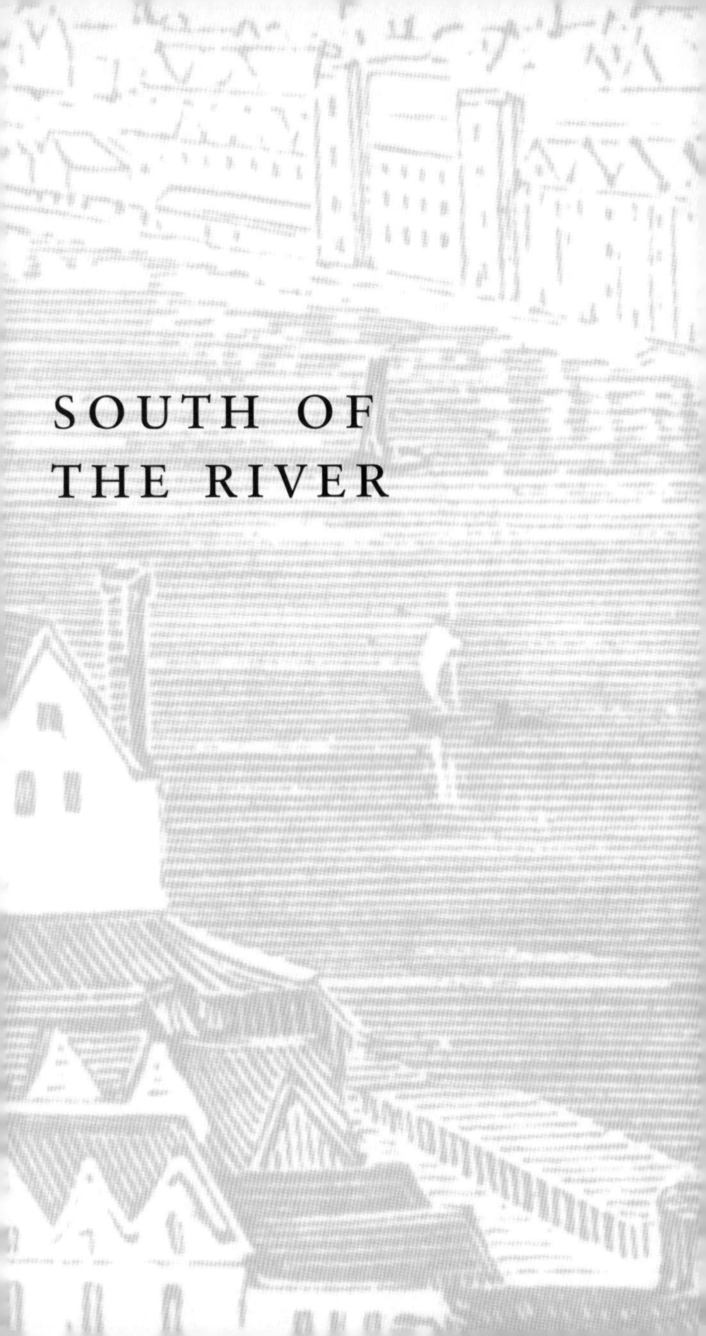

SOUTH OF THE RIVER

SOUTH OF THE RIVER

1 Battersea Park
2 Eversleigh Road
3 The Type Museum
4 Brockwell Park Lido
5 Dulwich Picture Gallery
6 Horniman Museum
7 Ringmore Rise
8 Bermondsey Market or the New Caledonian

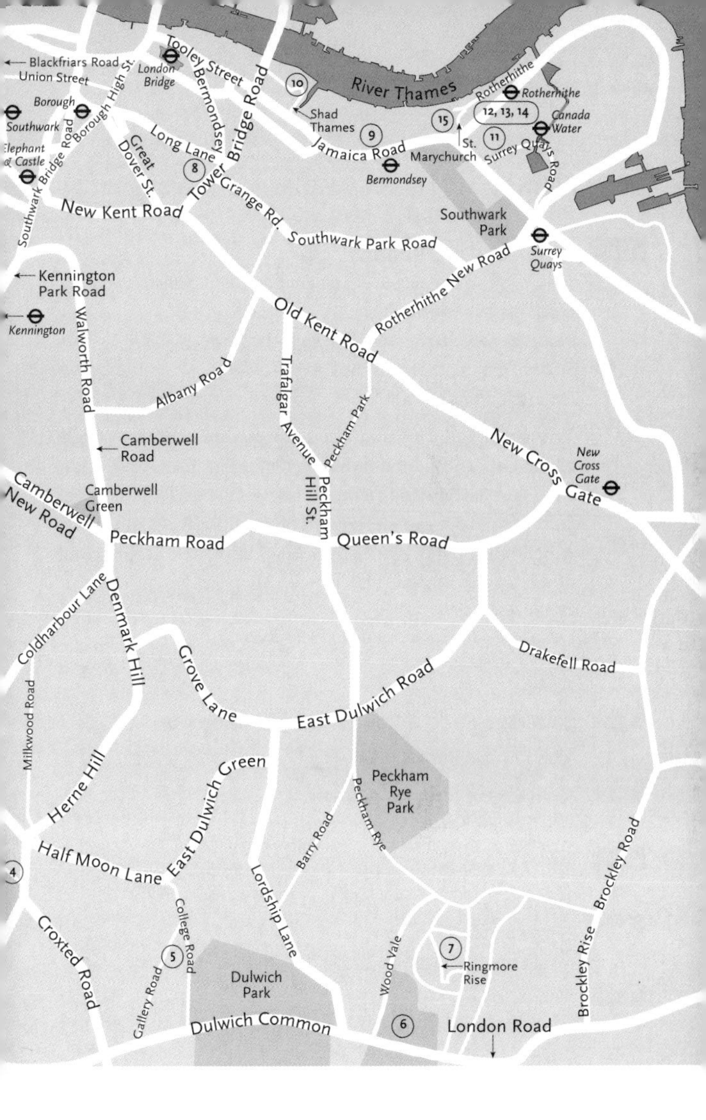

9 Rosie's
10 Design Museum
11 Canada Water Station
12 Thames Tunnel
13 St. Mary's Church
14 Mayflower Inn
15 Manor House

SOUTH OF THE RIVER

13.1 **Battersea Park Buddha**

1985, a gift to the people of London from the Japanese Buddhist Order Nipponzan Myohoji

Peace Pagoda, Battersea Park SW8, SW11

Sloane Square; then take bus #137

railway: Battersea Park, from Victoria

Two small, uplifting and often repeated pleasures: the sight of the Golden Buddha in his shrine in Battersea Park opposite Chelsea Embankment, and of a new arrival—the gold-starred azure onion dome of the little Russian church which improbably comes into view on the left as you come down off the M4 on the Chiswick flyover.

PETER CARSON

Publishing editor and translator from Russian

13.1 **Battersea Park: a Connoisseur's Afternoon**

Albert Bridge Road SW11

2.22 **Jeroboam's**

51 Elizabeth Street SW1, 020 7823 5623

2.23 **Henry Stokes & Co.**

58 Elizabeth Street SW1, 020 7730 7073

2.24 **Tomtom Ltd., Cigar Merchants**

63 Elizabeth Street SW1, 020 7730 1790

3.29 **Fulham News**

200 Fulham Road SW10, 020 7351 3435

There are very few "secrets" in such a busy, gossipy city as London, but there are some simple, unexploited pleasures. One of mine would be this. Take a car or a cab to Elizabeth Street in Belgravia where you will find a lot of what you need to nourish body and soul. At Jeroboam's, pick up some good bread and cheese and a bottle of better than average white burgundy: a 1996 Meursault would do fine. While the cab is waiting, nip into Henry Stokes's bookshop at number 58, a small village-like affair, but with a well-chosen stock of current titles. Buy something. In the same street Tomtom Ltd., Cigar Merchants, will sell you a Hoyo de Monterrey Epicure Number 2. Now divert the cab to Fulham Road where you will find the world's best newsagent, Fulham News. Buy an armful of your favourite papers and magazines, then have yourself dropped at the Chelsea Bridge entrance to Battersea Park. I love Battersea Park because of its oddness: built on spoil from the excavation of the Royal Docks, asparagus was cultivated here.

Anyway, select a bench overlooking the river, somewhere near the Buddhist Temple. On a weekday you will have the place entirely to yourself so, if you have remembered your running stuff, hide the food, papers and books and take a turn around the park's perimeter. This is about a mile and a half, so not too demanding, but enough to justify the indulgence of the food, drink, smoke and reading you are now going to enjoy.

The view from your bench is beautiful and evocative: this is Whistler's and Wilde's Thames. It is wonderful in warm sunshine, even lovelier in autumnal mist. From the bench, as you munch your bread and cheese and slurp the wine, you can enjoy one of the best urban views in Britain: Wren's dignified Royal Hospital and then the gorgeous red brick houses of Chelsea Embankment, these last Britain's most singular contribution to the history of world architecture. If you have brought two bottles, you can sit and wait and watch the sun go down over the eccentric Albert Bridge and the lumpy old Lots Road Power Station. For less than the price of a pretentious meal in a mediocre restaurant, you have had some of the very best London has to offer.

STEPHEN BAYLEY
Design consultant and author

13.2 Eversleigh Road

Battersea SW11

railway: Queen's Road Battersea, Clapham Junction

Eversleigh Road is part of the Shaftsbury Estate, south of and parallel to the railway line between Queen's Road Battersea and Clapham Junction stations. A wonderful example of early Victorian town planning for the working class.

PIERS PLOWRIGHT

Radio producer

13.3 The Type Museum

100 Hackford Road SW9, tel. 020 7735 0055

⊖ Stockwell, Oval

Tucked away in the back streets of Lambeth is the largest collection of typographic material in the world, in every written language. Visits by appointment.

KATY HOMANS

Graphic designer

A Suburban Drive: Upper Norwood

railway: Crystal Palace, from Victoria; Forest Hill, from Charing Cross

Church Road, Auckland Road, Belvedere Road

Upper Norwood SE19 (Not on map)

Stanley Hall

12 South Norwood Hill SE25, South Norwood (Not on map)

13.6 Horniman Museum

100 London Road SE23, ☎ 020 8699 1872, Forest Hill

13.7 Ringmore Rise

London is not a city in the European sense. It is rather an agglomeration of ever eliding suburbs with a tiny urban core. It is a precursor of Los Angeles, a horse-drawn, Victorian L. A. And, thus, its essence is to be found in those suburbs, which are captivating places to walk in and to drive around even if the notion of actually living in them is less appealing. Upper Norwood is an anthology of High Victorian Gothic domestic architecture—Church Road, Auckland Road, Belvedere Road are splendid sites of this style in its psychotic decadence. The curious may divert to South Norwood where the cutler W. F. Stanley (inventor of the vandal's weapon of choice, the Stanley Knife) designed and built the wonderfully bizarre Stanley Hall (12 South Norwood Hill SE25) in an idiom that has no precedent.

North of Norwood, at Forest Hill, the Horniman Museum is one of the very rare instances of a fine public building by an Arts and Crafts architect, C. Harrison Townsend. Behind it, from Ringmore Rise, a road of undistinguished houses of the early 1930s, are the best views of central London: one doesn't look across the city, one looks down on it.

JONATHAN MEADES
Writer, journalist and television performer

13.5 Dulwich Picture Gallery

1811–1815, Sir John Soane

College Road SE21, ☎ 020 8693 5254

railway: West Dulwich, from Victoria, followed by a fifteen-minute walk

Hidden away in the leafy suburbs of South London, within less than an hour's travel from the centre, is the world's seminal building in gallery design. In the early 19th century, Dulwich College School (founded by the Elizabethan actor Edward Alleyn) acquired the nucleus of an art collection, originally intended for the King of Poland, which included major works by Canaletto, Claude, Gainsborough, Poussin, Rembrandt, Rubens, Watteau, among others. The Regency architect Sir John Soane, presented with a limited budget, constructed between 1811–1815 one of the first custom-built public art galleries ever. He devised a masterpiece of abstract classicism in brick, dressed with Portland stone detailing, in which he pioneered a system of top-lighting. Recently restored, with a sensitively placed visitors' centre nearby, the gallery provides an afternoon's feast of architecture and painting in the arcadian setting of Dulwich village.

JOHN WILTON-ELY
Art historian

RECOMMENDED READING

Gillian Darley, *John Soane: An Accidental Romantic*, Yale University Press, 1999.
Giles Waterfield, 'Dulwich Picture Gallery' in exhibition catalogue, *John Soane, Architect: Master of Space and Light*, Margaret Richardson and Mary Anne Stevens, eds., Royal Academy of Arts, London, distributed by Yale University Press, 1999.

Only a short trip from London in a suburban village, which still retains its rural character, this fine collection of old masters (Rembrandt, Rubens, Van Dyck and others) is housed in a lovely Sir John Soane building. Drawing relatively few visitors, it is usually uncrowded so that you can view the paintings without someone at your elbow hoping you'll move on.

KENNETH SEEMAN GINIGER
Publisher

13.4 Brockwell Park Lido

Brockwell Park SE24

Brixton, then a ten- to fifteen-minute walk; railway: Herne Hill, from Victoria, Blackfriars, King's Cross

The Friday evening summer barbecues at Brockwell Park Lido, an outdoor swimming pool are a South London institution. Located between rarefied, rich, white Dulwich and full-on, predominantly-black Brixton, it's the place to come to see multicultural London at its most vibrant and enjoyable. Swim, lounge, read, chat, eat, or just people-watch—this is quintessential London: inclusive, frantic and fun.

JONATHAN COX
Editor

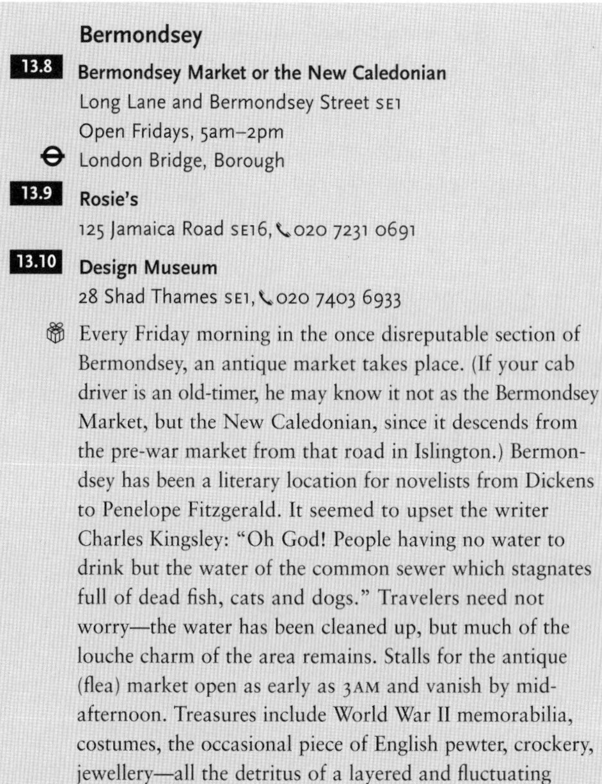

Bermondsey

13.8 **Bermondsey Market or the New Caledonian**
Long Lane and Bermondsey Street SE1
Open Fridays, 5am–2pm
London Bridge, Borough

13.9 **Rosie's**
125 Jamaica Road SE16, 020 7231 0691

13.10 **Design Museum**
28 Shad Thames SE1, 020 7403 6933

Every Friday morning in the once disreputable section of Bermondsey, an antique market takes place. (If your cab driver is an old-timer, he may know it not as the Bermondsey Market, but the New Caledonian, since it descends from the pre-war market from that road in Islington.) Bermondsey has been a literary location for novelists from Dickens to Penelope Fitzgerald. It seemed to upset the writer Charles Kingsley: "Oh God! People having no water to drink but the water of the common sewer which stagnates full of dead fish, cats and dogs." Travelers need not worry—the water has been cleaned up, but much of the louche charm of the area remains. Stalls for the antique (flea) market open as early as 3AM and vanish by mid-afternoon. Treasures include World War II memorabilia, costumes, the occasional piece of English pewter, crockery, jewellery—all the detritus of a layered and fluctuating island society, and all, we're assured by the vendors, at rock-bottom prices.

Include lunch at Rosie's; the savings will go a long way toward financing a splurge at The Ivy or The Square. Rosie seats you at communal tables, cheek to cheek with the teamsters, stall-keepers and patrons pulled in by the sales. Platters of fish and chips are passed from the kitchen over the packed tables, bottles of vinegar follow, and you leave dyspeptic, perhaps in time to consider a last memento—that moustache cup or Macallan water pitcher or Royal Fusiliers's saber.

After the market has closed, stroll the promenade at Butler's Wharf from London Bridge for a wonderful view of the city traffic on the Thames, or walk the Shad Thames beyond Tower bridge (used as the backdrop for David Lynch's *The Elephant Man*), and drop in on the Design Museum. A serendipitous day.

BRUCE DUCKER
Novelist

Canada Water Station to the Mayflower Inn

⊖ Canada Water

13.11 **Canada Water Station**
Surrey Quays Road SE16

13.12 **Thames Tunnel**
1825–1843, Sir Marc Brunel

13.13 **St. Mary's Church**
St. Marychurch Street SE16

13.14 **Mayflower Inn**
117 Rotherhithe Street SE16, ☎ 020 7237 4088

Take the extended Jubilee Underground line to Canada Water. The new station is surmounted by a large glass rotunda by Buro Happold (boldly restating in 1990s terms Charles Holden's iconic Arnos Grove Station of 1932–1933) and the adjacent bus station is a powerful and typical recent work by Eva Jiricna. Then take the East London line one stop to Rotherhithe. Leaving the platform you pass the entrance to Sir Marc Brunel's Thames Tunnel, called the "Great Bore" by *The Times* during its eighteen-year construction from 1825, but actually the great mother of all road and rail passages below water. At St. Mary's Church see the tomb of the Palau Prince Lee Boo, brought sightseeing to London from the Pacific in 1783 only to succumb almost immediately to smallpox. The gaunt 19th-century warehouses of this once important dockland area are now mostly converted to desirable riverside apartments.

Finally, stop for lunch in the picturesque Mayflower Inn (the ship began its voyage from Rotherhithe in 1620) where, on a jetty projecting above the Thames, you can enjoy unusually good pub food and fine Suffolk beer.
FRANK SALMON
Lecturer in art history

Richmond Park

Kingston Vale SW15, 020 8948 3209 (Not on map)
From tube, take bus #65 or #71.
Richmond

Richmond Park seems locked in *A Man for All Seasons* world of English oaks and huge antlered stags. Part formal plantation, part wild heath, its the best walking territory in London—especially in spring when the rhododendrons are in flower.
WILLIAM DALRYMPLE
Travel writer

Henry VIII Mound

Pembroke Lodge, Richmond Park (Not on map)
Richmond

This is London's most secret yet most dramatic view. Walk beneath the ancient oak trees and through the gardens of Pembroke Lodge to the top of the Mound. From there, on a clear day, you will see St. Paul's Cathedral, ten miles away, framed by trees as if through a key hole.
DAME JENNIFER JENKINS
President, Ancient Monuments Society

Richmond Half-Tide Weir

For information, phone Harbour Services, 020 7743 7900 (Not on map)
Richmond; railway: St. Margaret's, from Richmond

Every London guidebook recommends Richmond riverside, its magnificent 18th-century bridge, and the glorious curve

of the Thames under Richmond Hill and through Petersham Meadows. Richmond is also famous for high spring tides which submerge the cars of unsuspecting visitors. Less well-known is the device that preserves this riverscape when the tide ebbs. Walk a few hundred yards downstream from Richmond riverside, under Twickenham Bridge, and you come to a fine late Victorian hydraulic contraption (painted in cream and *eau-de-nil*) which combines four elements: a barge lock, a pedestrian footbridge, a set of rollers for punts and skiffs and three massive gantries holding 66-foot wide sluices. On the ebb tide these gates are lowered into place with a splash. They impound a five-foot depth of water. As the tide rises they're hoisted back into their gantry. A fine spectacle, twice daily.
MICHAEL HEBBERT
Professor

Rail Tour

If you open the London tube map you will notice that there is a line with no colour at all, and seemingly no logic to it either. Whereas others make a dash straight for the city centre, the North London line begins in the bottom left-hand corner at Richmond and throws a loop to terminate at the extreme right in North Woolwich. That's what I like about it. To long-suffering commuters it is the line from hell, but if time and the occasional cancellation is no object it provides one of the most unusual perspectives on London. I usually ride it from Acton to Highbury on the weekends that Arsenal are playing at home, past the old goods yard at King's Cross and Hampstead Heath. But if you carry on, you soon find yourself in the heart of London's East End and, if you take it in the opposite direction, Kew Gardens and the Public Record Office. Unlike the colour-coded lines, the NLL has few tunnels so if Silverlink has remembered to clean the windows you get a perfect view of "backdoor" London. Take a sandwich

for the inevitable delays and buy a day pass so you can get on and off. It is hard to think of a more authentic introduction to the city.
MARK HONIGSBAUM
Journalist and author

Kew Gardens

Royal Botanic Gardens, Kew, Richmond ☎ 020 8940 1171
(Not on map)
⊖ Kew Gardens

Waterlily House

1852, Richard Turner

Palm House

1844–1848, Decimus Burton

I find the Waterlily House, built in 1852, a small, strange oasis of warmth, and the Palm House, opposite, a place of serendipity. The underground aquarium, with its wonderful epigram—"without algae there can be no life on earth"—is a real surprise.
ROMESH GUNESEKERA
Author

During weekdays the canals are little frequented, except by occasional, unusually solitary fishermen. Except when a boat chugs by, there is total silence. My favourite of these walks is from Windmill Lane (with a remarkable road, rail and canal crossing) to Kew Gardens to view Hanwell Locks (six in all) to the vast canopied warehouse of Brent Meadows Wharf.
FRANCIS KING
Novelist and critic

RECOMMENDED READING
Anthony Burton and Derek Pratt, *Canal*, David and Charles, 1980.

Crystal Palace Park

1851–1854, Joseph Paxton
Sydenham Hill SE19 (Not on map)
railway: Crystal Palace, from Victoria

There have been dinosaurs at Crystal Palace since 1854 when Joseph Paxton created the park as a permanent home for the glass and iron building that housed the Great Exhibition. They survived the fire of 1936 which destroyed the Palace, but now their habitat is threatened again as the council embarks on a tree felling scheme. Campaigners against the building of a wholly inappropriate multiplex in another part of the park recently held a funeral for some two hundred of the doomed trees some of which are three hundred years old.

It is hoped that the dinosaurs will not be too exposed: one of the joys of encountering them is watching as children suddenly spot the enormous antlers of a megaceros—Irish elk—through the branches of trees, a massive iguanadon or a cluster of marine reptiles in a lagoon. The lakes, islands and thickets where these and others live form a geological time trail, constructed by distinguished experts of the day. If some of the models, sculpted by Waterhouse Hawkins to the instructions of Sir Richard Owen, Director of the Natural History Museum, are anatomically incorrect, they represent an important stage in our understanding of prehistoric life. They were created just ten years after the first discovery of dinosaur remains in Britain.

The vast fountains, the Atmospheric Railway, the aviators and balloonists, the Cup Finals, the visiting crowned heads are long gone but mementoes of the Crystal Palace's former glories, and of the fire, can be viewed in the charming and informative small museum on Anerley Hill, run by The Crystal Palace Foundation, an independent trust.

Other attractions in the park include the maze, a boating lake, a small zoo for children too young to appreciate its intrinsic sadness, a mini-railway, playground, visiting funfairs and fireworks displays, the Concert Bowl and the

National Sports Centre. If, however, you'd prefer a sweet and surreal celebration of the park on video, *The Pleasure Garden*, a short film directed in 1952 by James Broughton, photographed by Walter Lassally, stars Hattie Jacques as the magical *genius loci*, John Le Mesurier, Lindsay Anderson and Kermit Sheets. It won the *Prix du film de fantasie poetique* in Cannes in 1954.
SHENA MACKAY
Novelist

RECOMMENDED READING
Alan Ross Warwick, *The Phoenix Suburb: A South London Social History*, Norwood Society, 1991 (UK).

The views from up on the hill are some of the most exhilarating in London. The park's owners, the Borough of Bromley, have plans to restore much of its former glory, yet there's something enchanting about its current semi-dilapidated state. All that remains of the Palace are the long ballustraded promenades that formerly fronted it, and the rather battered sphinxes that once proudly stood sentinel over the world's most impressive greenhouse. The small Crystal Palace Museum nearby (only open on Sundays) tells the story of the Palace in Sydenham. It's housed in the old engineering school where John Logie Baird established his television company. And the television associations continue to this day—the towering Crystal Palace TV mast can be seen from as far afield as Hampstead Heath.

Further down the hill stands the Crystal Palace National Sports Centre (Ledrington Road, ☎ 020 8778 0131). The park has long established sporting connections. Motor races were held here from the 1930s to the 1970s, and, from 1895 to 1914, twenty Football Assocation Cup Finals were played in the park's grounds, attracting crowds of up to one hundred thousand. Continue to the bottom of the park to find the venerable old dinosaurs, peaking out from between the trees and lurking in the park's lakes!
JONATHAN COX
Editor

The Crystal Palace was removed from Hyde Park and re-erected at Sydenham after the Great Exhibition of 1851. It burnt down in November 1936. In the southeast corner of the now mostly trashed park that surrounded the building is one of London's strangest and most beguiling sites: a group of painted bronze verisimilar life-size statues of triceratops, iguanadon, pterodactyl and more. There are about fifteen of them, around a lake in a vaguely Japanese garden. To come upon them even when anticipating them is a near-hallucinatory experience. Which may not be what the sculptor Waterhouse Hawkins had in mind: they were more likely conceived and executed in a spirit of earnest didacticism. They are funny, frightening, perpetually uplifting.
JONATHAN MEADES
Writer, journalist and television performer

The Ice House

ca. 1830
Manor House Gardens, Lee, ☎ 020 8318 1358
(Not on map)
Open the first and third Sundays of the summer months
railway: take the overland train from Charing Cross, Waterloo East or London Bridge to Hither Green or Lee

On a very hot Sunday—the first or third Sunday between July and September—take an overland train to Lee or Hither Green. Walk through Manor House Gardens and find the set of metal steps which lead down to a brick built ice house and tunnel. Ice from the pond was packed into the well and kept for up to two years. Fruit and vegetables from the Manor House orchards and kitchen gardens were kept fresh in the adjoining chambers. Imagine the chilled flowers which were used as table decorations. A block of ice made a fountain as it slowly melted and spilled from the top of a tower of plates which displayed the flowers. Then climb back above ground and buy an ice cream from the kiosk.
CHRISSIE GITTINS
Poet and short story writer

RECOMMENDED READING
Sylvia P. Bearn and Susan Roach, *The Ice Houses of Britain*, Routledge, 1991.

River Walk: Beyond Tower Bridge

 Tower Bridge

13.15 **Manor House**
Rotherhithe Street SE16, 020 7237 3608

13.14 **Mayflower Inn**
117 Rotherhithe Street SE16, 020 7237 4088

For most people taking a Sunday stroll along the Thames Path, Tower Bridge is about as far east as they get. But accompany the river on its eastern journey past this exemplary Victorian carbuncle and things begin to get more interesting.

Beyond the depressing, soulless yuppie warehouse conversions of Butler's Wharf—ghostly communities gracing the river like something from a J. G. Ballard nightmare—lies Bermondsey, where you'll find a stately home, and beyond that in Rotherhithe, the history of America. Edward III's Manor House, admittedly a ruin now, lurks in a rather desultory spot opposite The Angel pub. Hyperactive kids are about the only people for whom its ruined walls have any contemporary relevance, but to think that an ancient seat of the English monarchy lies on a South London council estate is a wonderful thought, if for no other reason than to swell the south bank with a pride often dented by those north of the river.

Further up is Rotherhithe, a once industrious ship building community. It's a curious area—in the seventies it was a menacing National Front enclave, now just an odd mix of upwardly mobile riverfront wealth and inland council estates. Derek Jarman used to have his studio here, and much of his bleak anti-Thatcherite tirade *The Last of England* was filmed on this stretch of river. Walk along leafy Rotherhithe Street (the second longest street in London after Oxford Street), past warehouses more Dickensian than Dickens and you hit the Mayflower Inn.

It was from here that The Pilgrim Fathers set sail for the New World, and it's in the church opposite the pub that the returning crew of The Mayflower are buried.

If it's a sunny day, get yourself a pint and head on out to the deck at the back of the pub, where you can enjoy the open skies. The river affords a respite to London's oppressively claustrophobic architecture. If, as is more likely, the weather is traditionally British, book yourself in for a hearty Sunday roast and gaze at the impressive vista that is London's once thriving riverside.

DAN FOX
Writer and editor

BIOGRAPHIES

ROBERT KAHN is an architect in private practice. His work has been widely published. He has taught design, most recently at Yale University. In 1981 he was awarded the Prix de Rome by the American Academy in Rome. He lives with his wife Fiona in New York City and Shelter Island.

SIR JOHN SOANE'S MUSEUM was created by the architect Sir John Soane at No. 13 Lincoln's Inn Fields and has been a public museum since 1837. It survives as an integral whole, its interiors restored and its works of art displayed in the same authentic arrangements as they were in Soane's day. Many of its works of art, like the Hogarths, Canalettos and Turners, are of great pre-eminence—as are its architectural collections of books and drawings by the leading architects of the 17th and 18th. The Museum also holds changing exhibitions in its Soane Gallery. However, it still has the reputation of being a well-kept secret with the majority of its visitors hearing about it by personal recommendation. It is still, as Henry James described it in 1889, "one of the most curious things in London. . . illustrating the prudent virtue of keeping."

THE WHITECHAPEL ART GALLERY was founded in 1910 with the aim of bringing art to the people of East London. Now an internationally renowned independent gallery, the Whitechapel shows contemporary and modern art, both by well-known and local artists.

THE MUSEUM OF LONDON is the world's largest urban history museum and tells the story of London's archaeology, history and contemporary culture from earliest times to the present day. It maintains an active special exhibition programme as well as permanent galleries recording and documenting London's past.

INDEX OF RECOMMENDED READING

Peter Ackroyd, *Blake*, reissue, Minerva, 1996.

Peter Ackroyd, *Hawksmoor*, Penguin UK, 1993.

Toby Barnard and Jane Clark, eds., *Lord Burlington: Architect, Art and Life*, Hambledon London Ltd., 1994.

Morris Beakman, *The 43 Group*, Centreprise Publications, 1993 (US); 2000 (UK).

Geoffrey Beard, *The Work of Robert Adam*, John Bartholomew & Son, 1978.

Sylvia P. Bearn and Susan Roach, *The Ice Houses of Britain*, Routledge, 1991.

Simon Bradley and Nikolaus Pevsner, *London: The City Churches*, Penguin UK, 1998.

Simon Bradley and Nikolaus Pevsner, *The Buildings of England, London 1: The City of London*, Penguin, 1997.

Olivia Bristol and Leslie Geddes-Brown, *Doll's Houses*, Miller's Publications, 1997.

Anthony Burton and Derek Pratt, *Canal*, David and Charles, 1980.

Alan Crawford, *C.R. Ashbee: Architect, Designer and Romantic Socialist*, Yale University Press, 1986.

Roald Dahl, "The Mildenhall Treasure" in *The Wonderful Story of Henry Sugar and Six More*, Puffin Books, 1988.

Gillian Darley, *John Soane: An Accidental Romantic*, Yale University Press, 1999.

Dazed&Confused Magazine

Helen Dorey, "12–14 Lincoln's Inn Fields" in exhibition catalogue, *John Soane, Architect: Master of Space and Light*, Margaret Richardson and Mary Anne Stevens, eds., Royal Academy of Arts, London, distributed by Yale University Press, 1999.

Helen Dorey and Peter Thornton, *A Miscellany of Objects from Sir John Soane's Museum*, Laurence King, 1992.

Kerry Downes, *Hawksmoor*, Thames and Hudson, 1969.

James Dunnett and Gavin Stamp, eds., with preface by Charlotte Perriand, *Ernö Goldfinger: Works 1*, Architectural Association, 1983.

Robert Elwall, *Ernö Goldfinger*, RIBA Drawings Monographs, no. 3, John Wiley and Son Ltd., 1996.

David Esterly, *Grinling Gibbons and the Art of Carving*, Harry N. Abrams, 1998 (US); V&A Publications, 2000 (UK).

Freud Museum, *20 Maresfield Gardens: A guide to the Freud Museum*, Serpent's Tail, 1998.

Eileen Harris, *Osterley Park, Middlesex*, Official Guidebook, The National Trust, 1994.

Howard Hibbard, *Caravaggio*, Harper Collins, 1985.

Henry-Russell Hitchock and Philip Johnson, *The International Style*, reissue, W.W. Norton and Co., 1997.

Philip Hoare, *Noël Coward*, Simon & Schuster, 1996 (US); Random House, 1996 (UK).

Henry James, *A London Life*, Buccaneer Books, 1992.

M. R. James, *The Haunted Doll's House*, 2nd edition, Penguin, 2000

Paul Jeffrey, *The Parish Churches of Sir Christopher Wren*, Hambledon London Ltd., 1996.

Simon Jenkins, *England's Thousand Best Churches*, Allen Lane, The Penguin Press, 1999.

Johnnie Shand Kydd, *Spit Fire*, Violette Editions, 1997 (UK); Distributed Art Publications, 1997 (US).

Charles Lamb, "The Last Essays of Elia" in the *Collected Works of Charles Lamb*, Classic Books, 2000.

James Lees-Milne, *Earls of Curation: Five Great Patrons of 18th Century Art*, Penguin UK, 2001.

E.V. Lucas, ed., *The letters of Charles Lamb, to which are added those of his sister Mary Lamb*, J.M. Dent & Sons, Methuen & Co., 1935. o.p.

Ruth McClure, *Coram's Children, The London Foundling Hospital in the Eighteenth Century*, Yale University Press, 1981.

H. V. Morton, *In Search of London*, Methuen Publishing Ltd., 1988, o.p.

Ian Nairn, *Nairn's London*, Penguin UK, 1966, o.p. Later reissued with a new commentary: *Nairn's London: The Classic Guidebook*, revisited by Peter Gasson, Penguin, 1988.

Halina Pasierbska, *Doll's House Furniture*, Shire Publications Ltd., 1998.

Ronald Paulson, *Hogarth: His Life, Art and Times*, 2 vols., Yale University Press, 1971, o.p.

John Physick, *The Victoria and Albert Museum: The History of Its Building*, V&A Publications, 1982. o.p.

Kenneth Powell, *The Jubilee Line Extension*, Lawrence King, 2000.

Margaret Richardson and Mary Anne Stevens, eds., *John Soane, Architect: Master of Space and Light*, Royal Academy of Arts, London, distributed by Yale University Press, 1999.

Margaret Richardson, *66 Portland Place*, RIBA Publications, 1984.

Iain Sinclair, *Lights Out for the Territory*, Granta, 1997.

June Sprigg, *Shaker Design*, Whitney Museum of American Art, 1986.

Dorothy Stroud, *Sir John Soane, Architect*, Studio Books, 1961.

Alan Ross Warwick, *The Phoenix Suburb: A South London Social History*, Norwood Society, 1991.

Giles Waterfield, 'Dulwich Picture Gallery' in exhibition catalogue, *John Soane, Architect: Master of Space and Light*, Margaret Richardson and Mary Anne Stevens, eds., Royal Academy of Arts, London, distributed by Yale University Press, 1999.

Roger White, *Nicholas Hawksmoor and the Re-planning of Oxford*, Exhibition Catalogue, British Architectural Library Drawings Collection, Ashmolean Museum, Oxford, 1997.

David Widgery, *Some Lives! A GP's East End*, Simon and Schuster, 1993.

Colin St. John Wilson, *The Design and Construction of the British Library*, The British Library, 1998.

John Wilton-Ely, *Piranesi at the Soane Museum*, Azimuth Editions, 2001.

Patrick Wright, *A Journey Through Ruins*, Paladin, 1992.

INDEX OF CONTRIBUTORS

Tim Adams is a staff writer for the *Observer* where he was formerly Literary editor; prior to that he was Deputy Editor of Granta. He lives in Islington with his wife and daughter. pp. 20, 26, 134

Brian Allen is Director of Studies at the Paul Mellon Centre for Studies in British Art in London and Adjunct Professor of History of Art at Yale University. He is also a Fellow of the Society of Antiquaries of London. p. 123

Michael Arditti is a novelist, playwright and literary critic. His novels include *The Celibate* and *Easter*, which received Waterstone's Mardi Gras award. pp. 156, 220

John M. Ashworth is the Chairman of the British Library Board. He has been the Director of the London School of Economics (1990–96) and the government's chief scientist (1976–81). pp. 102, 144

Diana Athill was, for almost fifty years, a director of the publishing house André Deutsch Ltd., a career described in her recent memoir *Stet*. Her other publications include another memoir, *Instead of a Letter*, and a novel, *Don't Look at Me Like That*. p. 85

P. W. Atkins is Professor of Chemistry at Oxford University. He is the author of many widely used textbooks, and books on science for the general public. p. 78

Paul Baggaley was a bookseller in London for many years and is now a Director at the Harvill Press, for which he is presently producing a list of classic London novels. p. 171

Andrew Ballantyne is the author of *Architecture, Landscape and Liberty* and *What is Architecture?* He is Professor of Architecture at the University of Newcastle-upon-Tyne. pp. 34, 77

J. G. Ballard's many novels include *Crash*, *Cocaine Nights* and *Empire of the Sun*, which was based on his childhood in a Japanese internment camp and later made into a film by Steven Spielberg. p. 166

Michael Barker writes and lectures on art, architecture and decorative arts, and is co-author of *The North of France—A Guide to the Art, Architecture and Atmosphere of Artois, Picardy and Flanders*. pp. 58, 139

Nicola Barker, a novelist and short story writer, won the 2000 Impac Award—the world's richest prize for a single work of fiction—for her third novel, *Wide Open*. p. 215

Paul Barker writes widely on social and cultural issues and was formerly editor of the opinion weekly, *New Society*. He is Senior Research Fellow at the Institute of Community Studies, London. p. 204

Alan Baxter is the engineering designer of many new landmark buildings and is involved in the conservation of historic structures in London. p. 129

Stephen Bayley was responsible for The Design Museum and created The Boilerhouse Project at the V&A. His books include *Sex, Drink and Fast Cars*. He resigned in protest from the Millennium Dome project. p. 228

James Bettley was Head of Collection Development at the National Art Library, Victoria & Albert Museum, 1997–2000. He was previously at the British Architectural Library of the Royal Institute of British Architects and the Design Museum. p. 59

Lexy Bloom, formerly at *The New York Review of Books*, now works for *Granta* and The Little Bookroom in London. p. 33, 88

Roger Bowdler is the author of various articles and television documentaries on tombs. p. 175

Elliot Boyd, a member of the Royal Institute of British Architects, is an architect practicing in London. p. 157, 174

Gabriele Bramante is the Principal of Bramante Architects in London. p. 61

Alan Brownjohn is a poet. He has also published three novels, *The Way You Tell Them, The Long Shadows* and *A Funny Old Year*. p. 87

Edward Burd, an architect, was for thirty years a partner at Hunt Thompson Associates, where he worked primarily on conservation and social housing projects. He lectured at the Bartlett School of Architecture and was a RIBA External Examiner. He is now retired and divides his time between London and southwest France. pp. 40, 196, 217

James Campbell's books include *Talking at the Gates, A Life of James Baldwin* and *This Is the Beat Generation*. pp. 57, 82, 186

Peter Carson was formerly Editor-in-Chief at Penguin. Now retired, he works as a freelance editor and translator from Russian. pp. 68, 146, 228

Adam Chodzko is an artist, working primarily with video and photography. p. 102

Susannah Clapp is Theatre Critic of the *Observer* and the author of *With Chatwin*, a memoir of Bruce Chatwin. p. 129

Barry Clayton is an architect specialising in the conservation of historic buildings. His expertise in the works of Sir John Soane has led to his involvement in the restoration of the House and Entrance Gateway at Tyringham in Buckinghamshire, and the ongoing major reconstruction of Soane's last major country house, Pell Wall in Shropshire. p. 62

Michael Coveney is the Theatre Critic of the *Daily Mail* and author of several biographies, including those of Maggie Smith, Mike Leigh and Andrew Lloyd Webber. pp. 83, 212

Jonathan Cox is an editor, writer and photographer for *Time Out* City Guides. pp. 232, 239

William Dalrymple, an award-winning travel writer, is the author of *In Xanadu, City of Djinns, From the Holy Mountain* and *The Age of Kali*. pp. 176, 235

Gillian Darley's most recent book is a biography of Sir John Soane. She was co-author with Andrew Saint of *The Chronicles of London*, a historical anthology of London. pp. 52, 83, 117, 140, 193

Robyn Davidson is a London-based writer. Her books include *Tracks*, winner of the Thomas Cook Travel Book Award, and *Desert Places*, shortlisted for the same prize. p. 207

Giles de la Mare was director of Faber & Faber from 1969 to 1998, and is now the now the chairman of Giles de la Mare Publishers, founded in 1995. p. 140

Lesley Downer's books include *Geisha: The Secret History of a Vanishing World* and *On the Narrow Road to the Deep North*. She writes for *The Wall Street Journal Europe*. pp. 36, 125

Bruce Ducker is the author of six novels, including *Bloodlines* and *Lead Us Not Into Penn Station*. p. 233

James Dunnett, an architect and lecturer, translated Le Corbusier's *The Decorative Art of Today* in 1986. pp. 64, 219

Robert Dye RIBA is an architect who has worked with Sir James Stirling and Fred Koetter. p. 146

Geoffrey Elborn, a biographer and critic, has written lives of Edith Sitwell and Francis Stuart. He is currently writing about Patricia Highsmith. pp. 72, 131

Duncan Fallowell is the author of two travel books, *To Noto* and *One Hot Summer in St. Petersburg*. His most recent novel is *A History of Facelifting*. pp. 20, 39, 53, 168, 174

Lex Fenwick is the Managing Director—Europe, Bloomberg LP. p. 101

Michele Field represents Australian arts organisations in Britain and is a London correspondent for Australian newspapers and magazines. pp. 108, 110

Ophelia Field is a biographer, Books Consultant to *The Sunday Telegraph* and a policy analyst in the field of refugees and human rights. She is currently writing a biography of Sarah, Duchess of Marlborough (1660–1744). p. 109

Mary Flanagan, an American writer and critic living in London, is the author of three novels (*Trust, Rose Reason* and *Adèle*) and two collections of short stories (*Bad Girls* and *The Blue Woman*). p. 213

Leslie Forbes is a broadcaster and writer whose books include *Fish, Blood & Bone*, a mystery set in London and Tibet. p. 209

Dan Fox is assistant editor of *frieze* magazine, and a freelance critic and film maker. pp. 22, 206, 241

Christopher Frayling is Rector of the Royal College of Art. A broadcaster and cultural historian, his books include *Sergio Leone –Something to Do With Death*, *The Art Pack* and *The Face of Tutankhamun*. pp. 90, 211

Philip French is the *Observer's* film critic, author of *Westerns* and co-editor of *The Faber Book of Movie Verse*. p. 91

Jay Anthony Gach is a composer of concert music and music for the media. pp. 132, 143

Dr. Claire Gapper is a specialist in early decorative plasterwork in England, having completed her PH.D thesis on the subject at the Courtauld Institute of Art in 1998. p. 141

Jeremy Garfield-Davies is a director and furniture expert at Mallett, the antique dealers. He advises on the research, restoration and acquisition of English furniture for some of the most important private collections worldwide. pp. 37, 39

Christopher Geelan and Sarah Gordon run the London-based Young Shakespeare Theatre Company. p. 193

Kenneth Seeman Giniger is a book publisher, editor and anthologist in New York City. pp. 74, 232

Janine di Giovanni was named Foreign Correspondent of the Year for 2000, as well as winning the Amnesty International Award and the National Magazine Award. She works for *The Times* covering wars in the Balkans, Asia, Africa, Latin America and the Middle East. pp. 165, 168

Chrissie Gittins is a poet. She is currently Writer-in-Residence for Maidstone Borough Council. p. 240

Victoria Glendinning is a prize-winning biographer and journalist. Her books include lives of Vita Sackville-West, Trollope, and Jonathan Swift, and the novel *Electricity*. pp. 18, 69

Antony Gormley, a sculptor, is the creator of the Angel of the North. He was awarded the Turner Prize in 1994. p. 96

Nicci Gerrard and Sean French, both journalists, write thrillers together, including *Killing Me Softly* and *The Safe House*. p. 194

Ron Gray is the author of books on Goethe, Kafka, Brecht, and Ibsen, and also on Cambridge gardens and Cambridge street names. p. 69

Romesh Gunesekera was born in Sri Lanka and now lives in London. His first novel, *Reef*, was shortlisted for the Booker Prize and was awarded a Premio Mondello Prize in Italy. His most recent novel, *The Sandglass*, received the inaugural BBC Asia Award. pp. 167, 198, 237

David Hare is an award-winning writer and director. His 22 plays include *Plenty*, *The Judas Kiss*, *Amy's View* and *The Blue Room*. p. 185

Ronald Hayman's books include biographies of Nietzsche, Kafka, Brecht, Sartre, Proust, Thomas Mann and Jung. pp. 184, 189

Janeen Haythornthwaite is an art historian who works for the

Whitechapel Gallery and the Tate Modern. Rick Haythornthwaite is CEO of Bluecircle Industries. p. 42

Edwin Heathcote is an architect and writer in London. He is the author of a number of books including *Theatre: London* and is the editor of *Church Building* magazine. pp. 26, 138

Michael Hebbert, author of *London, More by Fortune than Design*, is a historian, geographer and town planner who lives in London and Manchester. He heads the School of Planning and Landscape at the University of Manchester. pp. 221, 235

Angela Hederman is editor and publisher at The Little Bookroom in New York. p. 112

Dave Hill is a journalist and author of books on pop music, politics, football and gender issues. He lives near the Narrow Way with his wife and five children. p. 216

Philip Hoare lives in Hoxton, London. His books include biographies of Stephen Tennant and Noël Coward, *Wilde's Last Stand* and *Spike Island*. He was co-curator of *Icons of Pop:* 1958–1999 at the National Portrait Gallery. pp. 45, 143, 208

Phil Hogan writes a weekly column for the *Observer*. His first novel is called *Hitting the Groove*. p. 154

Peter J. Holliday is a historian of classical art and archaeology at California State University. He lived in London when he was a graduate student and is now a frequent visitor. pp. 111, 170

Katy Homans is a graphic designer living in New York. p. 230

Mark Honigsbaum is a journalist and the former chief reporter for the *Observer*; he is also a broadcaster and author of *The Fever Trail—Malaria, The Mosquito and The Quest for Quinine*. p. 236

Peter Horrocks, a barrister, is a freeman of the City of London. He is the Chairman of the Sherlock Holmes Society of London, runs the Covent Garden Minuet Company, an 18th century dance group, is a Fellow of the Royal Asiatic Society and is a player of real tennis. p. 12, 39

Peter Howard, an architect, is co-author of guides to the architecture of Oxford and Cambridge. p. 55

David Hughes is an award-wining crime writer, living in London. p. 18

Lucy Hughes-Hallet is the author of *Cleopatra*, winner of the Fawcett prize. She is currently writing a book on heroes and hero-worship. pp. 52, 84, 153

Johanna Hurwitz is the award-winning author of more than fifty popular children's books. She lectures to students, teachers, parents and librarians from Mississippi to Mozambique. p. 15

Nicholas Hytner is a London-based theatre and film director. p. 43

Ian Jack has edited *Granta* since 1995. He was a reporter for the *Sunday Times* between 1970 and 1986, and co-founder of the *Independent on Sunday* in 1989. In Britain, his awards include those for reporter, journalist and editor of the year. He lives with his family in London. p. 221

Bernard Jacobson has had a gallery in London for more than 30 years, initially publishing prints and subsequently dealing in modern and contemporary British and American art. p. 194

Dame Jennifer Jenkins is President of the Ancient Monuments and formerly Chair of the National Trust, the Consumers Association and the Historic Buildings Council for England. pp. 69, 235

Robert Kahn is an architect in private practice in New York and the Series Editor of City Secrets guidebooks. p. 32

Ian Kelly is an actor and writer. His publications include *Shakespeare Cinema*. pp. 124, 192

Francis King was drama critic of the *Sunday Telegraph*. His books include *Act of Darkness*, *The Domestic Animal* and *Dead Letters*. He was the winner of the Somerset Maugham Prize, the Katherine Mansfield Prize and Yorkshire Post Novel of the Year Award. pp. 170, 237

Susan Kleinberg, an artist, has exhibited at the Venice Biennale, the American Center in Paris and the Castelli Gallery. pp. 21, 111

Phillip Knightley is an author and a journalist. His latest book is *Australia: A Biography of a Nation*. He has lived in Notting Hill for 35 years. p. 167

Zachary Leader is a Professor of English Literature at the University of Surrey Roehampton and the author and editor of books on Romantic poetry and 20th century British fiction. His most recent publication is *The Letters of Kingsley Amis*. Though an American, he has lived in London for more than thirty years. p. 51

Penelope Lively is a novelist and short story writer. She was born and grew up in Egypt and now lives in London. p. 130

Robert Livesey, an architect, is director of the Knowlton School of Architecture at Ohio State University. pp. 42, 84, 115, 196, 204, 220

George Loudon is Chairman of Helix Associates Ltd and a Director of CMG PLC. p. 36

Felicity Lunn is an independent curator and lecturer; she was formerly Curator at the Whitechapel Art Gallery. pp. 133, 196

Fiona MacCarthy is a cultural historian and author of biographies of Eric Gill and William Morris. She is writing the life (and after-life) of Byron. pp. 44, 63, 156, 184

Shena Mackay is a fellow of the Royal Society of Literature and a distinguished visiting Professor at Middlesex University. Her books include *The World's Smallest Unicorn*, *Dunedin* and the Booker-shortlisted *The Orchard on Fire*. p. 238

Angus MacQueen's documentary work includes *The Death of Yugoslavia*, which won a British Acadamy Award, and *Dancing for Dollars*, which received an Emmy. pp. 59, 197

Imogen Magnus has worked as a theatre designer and costume designer in films and television. She now writes on historic gardens and teaches. pp. 108, 142

Patrick Marber is a writer and director. His plays include *Dealer's Choice* and *Closer*. pp. 75, 122

Charles Marsden-Smedley is a museum and exhibition designer. pp. 61, 87

Brian Masters writes about crime and art. His 23 books include *Killing for Company*, which won the Gold Dagger Prize for non-fiction in 1985. He is also an authority on gorillas and dukes. pp. 41, 141

Carol McDaid is an editor and journalist on the *Observer*. p. 70

Andrew Mead is a staff writer for *The Architects' Journal*, contributing there and elsewhere on architecture, art and landscape. pp. 82, 187

Jonathan Meades is a filmmaker and critic, writing on architecture and food. His books include *Filthy English*, *Peter Knows what Dick Likes*, and *Pompey*, a novel. A new novel, *Fowler Family Blood*, is published in 2001. He won the Essay Prize at the Paris International Arts film Festival in 1994 and the Glenfiddich Trophy in 1998. pp. 230, 240

Roger Michell is a film and theatre director of, among others, *Persuasion* and *Notting Hill*. p. 191

David Miles is the Chief Archaeologist of English Heritage and lives on Millbank overlooking the Thames. pp. 21, 38

David Mlinaric, a partner at Mlinaric, Henry and Zervudachi, is an interior designer and decorator. He has worked on various museums and heritage sights in London and abroad, including The National Gallery, The Royal Opera House and several British embassies, as well as on many private houses and flats around the world. pp. 76, 115

Lucinda Montefiore is a writer and radio producer. pp. 71, 166

Deborah Moggach is a writer of screenplays and novels that include *Close Relations* and *Tulip Fever*. pp. 145, 191, 205

Wendy Moonan is the antiques columnist for *The New York Times*, architecture editor of *House & Garden*, and president of the Sir John Soane's Museum Foundation. p. 117

Rowan Moore is architecture critic of the *Evening Standard*. He was editor of the architecture magazine *Blueprint* and founding partner of Zombory-Moldovan Moore Architects. Publications include *Vertigo, The Strange New World of the Contemporary City* and *Building Tate Modern*. p. 216

Fidelis Morgan, writer and actor, is the author of *Unnatural Fire*, a whodunit set in 1699 London. She is a specialist in 17th- and 18th-century English theatre history. pp. 24, 50

Carole Morin has been writer-in-residence at Wormwood Scrubs prison and Literary Fellow at the University of East Anglia. Her books include *Lampshades*, *Dead Glamorous* and *Penniless in Park Lane*. pp. 72, 76

Patrick Morreau is a retired consulting engineer. p. 71

Nicholas Mosley, novelist and biographer, won the Whitbread Book of the Year Award in 1990 for *Hopeful Monsters*. p. 195

Andrew Motion is the Poet Laureate and Professor of Creative Writing at the University of East Anglia. p. 148

Peter Murray, Director of Wordsearch Ltd., was founding publisher of *Blueprint*, *Tate* and *Eye—The International Review of Graphic Design*. He was the curator of "New Architecture—The Work of Foster Rogers Stirling" and "Living Bridges", exhibitions at the Royal Academy. p. 179

Jeremy Musson, an architectural historian, is Architectural Editor of *Country Life* and author of *The English Manor House*. He was born in London in 1965 and as a child lived on the Abbey Road made famous by the Beatles. pp. 35, 138, 210

Richard Noble lives in London. He writes about political philosophy from the 18th century to the present and the contemporary visual arts. p. 98

Al Orensanz is the author of five books on sociology and semiology in urban communities. pp. 45, 164

Nadine Orenstein is an Associate Curator in charge of the German and Netherlandish Old Master prints in The Metropolitan Museum of Art, New York. pp. 13, 41

Cornelia Parker, artist, is known for a number of large installations including *Cold Dark Matter: An Exploded View* where she suspended the fragments of a garden shed, blown up for her by the British Army, which was exhibited at the Tate Modern. Shortlisted for the 1997 Turner Prize, she has had major solo exhibitions in London, Paris, New York, Boston, Chicago and Philadelphia. pp. 206, 209

Ruth Pavey has lived and worked in London for 25 years, teaching art and English to inner-city children. She writes for national publications on contemporary fiction, crafts and horticulture. pp. 97, 99, 118, 199

Clayre Percy works for The Landmark Trust on environmental research and libraries and is Trustee of the Lutyens Trust. She is editor of Edwin Lutyens's letters to his wife. p. 153

Piers Plowright, who retired from BBC Radio in 1997 after 30 years as a producer, is a winner of several Prix Italia for Radio Documentary and of several Sony awards. He is fellow of the Royal Society of Literature, a freelance-radio producer and a part-time lecturer in radio. pp. 144, 215, 230

Peter Porter, an Australian-born poet, won the Whitbread Prize in 1987. He has lived in Paddington in London since 1960. p. 12

Peter Powell is a London historian and he leads Angel Walks in Islington. A professional actor and singer, he has lived in Islington for 30 years. Other Angel Walks include those on Charles Dickens, Joe Orton, and walks in Highgate and Hampstead. pp. 133

Anne Purchas M.A. is an architectural historian and a free-lance lecturer and writer on architectural and garden history for various journals. pp. 55, 56

Theodore K. Rabb is a Professor of History at Princeton University. The author or editor of more than a dozen books, he is a contributor to *The New York Times*, the *TLS*, and other publications. pp. 13, 36

Michael Ratcliffe was the Literary Editor of *The Times* and Theatre Critic of the *Observer*. He now writes about travel for *The New York Times*. pp. 127, 152

Margaret Richardson has been the curator of Sir John Soane's Museum since 1995. She is the president of the Twentieth Century Society and is a specialist in architectural drawings. Her books include *Architects of the Arts and Crafts Movement* and *Sketches by Lutyens*. pp. 68, 107

Alan Ross (1922–2001) was Editor of the *London Magazine* and author of memoirs, poems, travel books and biographies. pp. 90, 176

Glen Roven, four-time Emmy winner, lives in London and New York City. His first Broadway musical opens in the fall of 2001. pp. 159, 213

Frank Salmon is a Lecturer in the History of Art at the University of Manchester and author of *Building on Ruins: The Rediscovery of Rome and English Architecture*. p. 234

Miranda Sawyer is a journalist and broadcaster. She is the author of *Park and Ride*, a personal history of suburbia. p. 23

Ann Saunders worked on the restoration of Lambeth Palace Library after the war. Her books include *Regent's Park* and *Art and Architecture of London* and *St. Paul's Cathedral*. She is editor of *London Topographical Society* and *Costume Society*. p. 218

Jon Savage is a historian of popular culture. He is the author of *England's Dreaming: Sex Pistols and Punk Rock*. p. 178

Marjorie M. Scardino is Chief Executive of Pearson PLC, owners of The Financial Times Group, The Penguin Group and RTL Television. pp. 32, 59, 64

Lynda Schor is the author of *Appetites* and *True Love & Real Romance*, two books of short fiction. She teaches fiction writing at the New School University. p. 14

Miranda Seymour is a biographer, novelist and critic. She also writes a weekly column on herbs and their uses for the *Independent*. pp. 63, 175

Shez 360, an artist, has exhibited widely in London and at the Whitechapel Art Gallery, The Tate Modern, and abroad with the British Council. pp. 77, 206

Alexandra Shulman is the editor of *Vogue* in London. pp. 52, 167

Susan Silberberg-Pierce is a classical art historian and photographer of ancient sites. p. 111

Clive Sinclair, born in London, is the author of four novels, including *Blood Libels* and *Cosmetic Effects*. He is a winner of the Somerset Maugham Award and the PEN MacMillan Silver Pen. pp. 127, 169

Mark Sladen is a curator at the Barbican Centre in London. He also writes for magazines including *frieze* and *Tate*. p. 26

John Slyce writes on contemporary art and culture from his home in east London. pp. 126, 218

Charles Saumarez Smith is Director of the National Portrait Gallery and lives in Stepney. pp. 205, 219

Neil Spencer is a journalist and scriptwriter. He is the co-writer of a trilogy of short films on London: *Paris Brixton*, *Sari and Trainers* and *Soul Patrol*. p. 99

Ralph Steadman is a cartoonist, illustrator, printmaker and writer. He has illustrated such classics as *Alice in Wonderland* and created prints on writers from William Shakespeare to William Burroughs. In addition, he has written books on Sigmund Freud and Leonardo da Vinci, and collaborated with Hunter S. Thompson on *Fear and Loathing in Las Vegas*. p. 56

Lucretia Stewart is the author of *Tiger Bam: Travels in Laos, Vietnam and Cambodia* (1992); *The Weather Prophet: A Caribbean Journey* (1995); and *Making Love: A Romance* (1999). She is the editor of *Erogenous Zones: An Anthology of Sex Abroad* (2000). pp. 90, 134

Lady Stirling (aka Mary Shand) is a furniture and interior designer. She is the widow of Sir James Stirling, the architect, and they have one son and two daughters. pp. 17, 20, 112, 125, 147, 154

Susan Swan, a novelist, has had her fiction published in ten countries. Her last novel, *The Wives of Bath*, was a *Guardian* fiction finalist. The film *Lost and Delirious*, based on this novel, has been chosen for the premiere selection at Sundance 2001. p. 16

A. A. Tait, a professor of art history at the University of Glasgow, is the author of two books on Robert Adam, the architect, and on landscape architecture. A trustee of several museums and institutions, he lives in Scotland and London and has been married to a New Yorker for the last forty years. They have two children. pp. 19, 164

Emma Tennant was born in London and grew up in the borders of Scotland. Her new novel *Sylvia and Ted* will be published by Henry Holt in the U.S.A. (2001). She is a fellow of the Royal Society of Literature. pp. 164, 169

Simon Thurley was curator of the Historic Royal Palaces for eight years before taking up a post as Director of the Museum of London. He is an authority on 16th- and 17th-century English architecture. pp. 42, 205

Eva Tucker's novels include *Contact* and *Drowning*. She writes for radio and various magazines and newspapers, and she translated Joseph Roth's *The Radetzky March* for Allen Lane, The Penguin Press. p. 86

Mario Vargas Llosa, the Peruvian writer and politician, is author of *The Time of the Hero*, *The Green House*, *Conversation in the Cathedral*, and *The War of the End of the World*, among other novels. He is also the author of noteworthy criticism. In 1990 he ran unsuccessfully for the Peruvian presidency. p. 103

Erica Wagner was born in New York and lives in London where she is Literary Editor of *The Times*. Her books are *Gravity: Stories* and *Ariel's Gift: Ted Hughes, Sylvia Plath and the Story of Birthday Letters*. pp. 123, 147

Marina Warner is a writer of fiction and history. Her most recent study of mythology is *No Go the Bogeyman: Scaring, Lulling and Making Mock*. Her newest novel is *The Leto Bundle* . pp. 96, 187

Tim Willis works for various British newspapers and magazines. He is also "Interesting Britain" correspondent for travelintelligence.net. pp. 172, 173

John Wilton-Ely, an art historian, is a Fellow of the Society of Antiquaries and the Royal Society of Arts. He is the author of *Piranesi as Architect and Designer*. pp. 116, 177, 231

Cecilia Wong, formerly of Cecilia Wong Designs, Los Angeles, is an interior designer and art historian. She lives in London. p. 54

Roger Woodley is a Lecturer at University College London in architecture and author of the *London Blue Guide*. p. 145

Gaby Wood is a journalist and critic. Her books include *Living Dolls: A History of the Quest for Mechanical Life*. pp. 73, 157

Karen Wright is the editor of *Modern Painters* and co-editor of the *Penguin Book of Art Writing*. pp. 155, 211

Nick Wyke is a journalist at *The Times* and has recently devised a walking tour of Pimlico in London. pp. 35, 41, 43, 51

GENERAL INDEX

MORE BOOKS FROM THE LITTLE BOOKROOM

City Secrets Rome
Edited by Robert Kahn
ISBN 1-892145-04-9

City Secrets Florence, Venice & the Towns of Italy
Edited by Robert Kahn
ISBN 1-892145-01-4

Upcoming volumes in the City Secrets series: *City Secrets New York, City Secrets Amsterdam, City Secrets Berlin, City Secrets Las Vegas, City Secrets Los Angeles, City Secrets North Carolina*

Artists in Residence
by Dana Micucci
ISBN 1-892145-00-6

Historic Restaurants of Paris
by Ellen Williams
ISBN 1-892145-03-0

Here is New York
by E. B. White with a new introduction by Roger Angell
ISBN 1-892145-02-2

Harpo Speaks . . . about New York
by Harpo Marx with Rowland Barber
Introduction by E. L. Doctorow
ISBN 1-892145-06-5

The Impressionists' Paris
Walking tours of the artists's studios, homes and the sites they painted
by Ellen Williams
ISBN 0-9641262-2-2

Picasso's Paris
Walking tours of the artist's life in the city by Ellen Williams
ISBN 0-9641262-7-3

In 2002:

Rome from the Ground Up
A traveler's guide to history, art and architecture
by James H. S. McGregor
ISBN 1-892145-11-1

The Public Gardens of New York City
by Nancy Berner and Susan Lowry
ISBN 1-892145-20-0